D1492345

ONE
A cook and her cupboard

FLORENCE KNIGHT

Photographs by Jason Lowe

Contents

One: Olive Oil

Two: Flour

Three: Mustard

Eight: Eggs

Nine: Honey

Ten: Chocolate

The kitchen cupboard

I grew up in a house in the country called Pinewood Cottage. The larder there was a large wooden cabinet lined with old newspapers. It was always filled to the brim: canned peaches that we'd won at a tombola stall, sticky honey pots, old jars of homemade mince meat, open cereal boxes, split pasta bags, crusty-edged bottles of ketchup and mustard. The entire contents were placed Jenga-like and you had to prise open the door in a very particular way. When you got inside, you had to be careful that the contents didn't tumble onto your toes while also fending off cats and dogs looking optimistically for another meal. It was precarious. It was chaotic. The larder is where it all started.

It wasn't a strict home and we were a happy, boisterous family. Mumma was often frantic with six hungry mouths to feed. She would be the first to admit that she's not the greatest cook. She didn't have the will, patience or time. She's a petite woman with wild curly red hair. She was always very supportive, teaching me sewing, art and literature. Not so much about cooking.

Corners were always cut. A roux was made by pouring flour over cooked pasta, then adding butter and milk later. Onions were 'cut' with the bluntest knife possible. It normally worked out ok in the end, but from an early age I realised I could help. 'Mumma, what are you doing?'

Although I was the second youngest of five, as soon as I could push a chair up against the stain-covered oven, I was interfering and experimenting with food. My first culinary adventure was 'Baked Bean Pie'. I still remember pouring the boiling hot water over the chalky white granules of Smash, and watching in amazement as they ballooned into fluffy clouds of fake potato.

I hated school dinners though. My little sister Primrose and I would often go without, to save our one pound dinner money. By home time, we would be starving. Mum would be waiting, brandishing a white paper bag containing two iced buns, and we'd bicker over who got the one that wasn't stuck to the inside of the bag.

Pancake day with Mumma was an explosion of flour, eggs and burnt batter. Dad was more meticulous and organised in the kitchen, preparing the most perfectly-cut Marmite sandwiches with salt and vinegar crisps wedged inside. He was also more adventurous with flavours. He ate everything. Mouldy bread and cheese was 'penicillin', while prawn heads were 'calcium'. He'd stick the prawn heads on the ends of his fingers to tease us, then suck and slurp on their insides before gulping them down.

Nothing went to waste. The excess fat from roasts would be drained off and spread over bread the next day. The brown meat jelly looked like cat food, and Dad would have it dangle and wobble over his lips while making agreeable noises. On holidays, he fancied himself as an artist and would arrange a plate in the form of a face, using salami, cheese, cucumber and tomato.

Food was a humble thing in our house. There were never any individual plates. We shared everything. There was a farm shop nearby where we'd pick up fruit and veg, and buy warm loaves of bread that had just come out of the ovens. Eggs were gathered everyday from our chickens at the bottom of the garden. We tried to grow our own herbs and vegetables but rosemary was the only thing that survived the deer that roamed around freely.

The kitchen was what brought my family together. 'We're home!' We'd pour into the kitchen, and Mumma would barely wipe the large old battered table before plonking the food down. We ate like a pack of wild animals. A steaming bowl of green soup would be ladled out, and I'd find a huge piece of potato that had escaped Mum's blender, and sometimes a dog hair too that I would have to tease out of my mouth later. We'd still squabble over the last spoonfuls.

Dad died unexpectedly when I was in my teens. He had been a huge source of inspiration to me. I used the money he left me to train as a chef and went straight to work after graduating. Cooking was, and still is, a way for me to escape the pain of his loss.

I didn't know anyone in London, but I wanted to be alone, and the kitchen soon became my home from home. I was sad and very angry that my dad had been taken from us, and although I didn't know it at the time I needed a way of turning those feelings into something positive.

The kitchen was like being part of a busy dysfunctional family. There was no time to worry about life on the outside, and we barely had the chance to experience it in any case. Life as a chef is all-consuming. Which is not to say that the first kitchens I worked in were friendly places. They could be terrifying. They are often sterile and cold, populated by tough, motley characters. I didn't meet very many people who had a real love for food, and on the rare occasions when I did, they became friends for life. You need to earn people's respect and trust in a kitchen. This can take some time.

At the beginning, I was peeling sacks of potatoes and vast quantities of fragile soft-boiled eggs. I knew I needed experience, and that this would be lowly-paid or even unpaid. I used to turn up at the door of kitchens where I admired the chef's work, holding my roll of knives, and ask to work for free. I purposefully moved around, staying about a year in each kitchen. I always attached myself to the person I thought was the best chef, even if this meant getting in extra-early, or cleaning their section. It's exhausting after long shifts. I would often leave feeling like I was moving in slow motion while everyone around me was running at double speed.

I'm dyslexic and found conventional schooling a challenge, but the visual and practical side of cooking came naturally to me. I was instantly excited by the work, and that feeling has never left me. In fact, my work has become a complete obsession. I'm told I even talk about it in my sleep.

In the summer of 2009, a waitress tipped me off that there might be a promising job. After a quick trial on a quiet Sunday morning, I was offered the position of Head Chef at Polpetto, a new restaurant above The French House on Dean Street in Soho. I didn't know it then, but The French House and its dining room have an iconic status amongst the Soho fraternity, and foodies in general. The renowned Fergus Henderson had been a previous incumbent before he opened his restaurant St John's. The list of regulars reads like a 'Who's Who' of the great and the good of British artistic and literary life.

The restaurant was meticulously pieced together with a rusty tin ceiling, red banquettes, old bentwood chairs and miscellaneous antique light fittings. Even the crockery was a jumble of second-hand oddments and flowery patterns that were similar to the china I was collecting at home. The restaurant was a beautiful little gem, and I could tell from the start that it was a place I could make my own.

It was a refreshing change to work with people who were as passionate and excited about food as I am. Their enthusiasm for Venice and Venetian cooking traditions, in particular, was infectious and after a few trips to that beautiful city I also caught the bug.

The fish market in Venice has been around for some 500 years, and sits just beyond the Rialto Bridge in the heart of the city. I first encountered the market on a bitterly cold and damp morning in early February, before the Carnevale. It was freezing cold, but I quickly forgot about that as I tried to take in as much of the uniquely beautiful city as I could.

I went from stall to stall. I'd never seen so many species. Many came straight from the swamp pools that surround Venice. 'Canoce', for instance, are a local type of sweet crayfish, unlike anything I had seen or eaten before. The razor clams were tiny, as small as my little finger, and much sweeter and more flavoursome than the full-grown variety I had eaten in England. The soft-shelled crabs were alive and sold by the bucket-load. The trestle tables were buckling under the weight of octopus, squid, sea bream, mackerel, tuna, sardines and any number of other fish.

After the market I toured some of the more prestigious 'bacari' that dot the city. A 'bacaro' is a small Venetian wine bar that sells 'cichetti' – small bite-sized morsels designed to fill a hole between breakfast and lunch, or indeed lunch and dinner. These canteens are firmly embedded in the local fishing and trading traditions, bringing together all types of people. All are welcome, and this sense of egalitarianism and accessibility, which were already essential elements in my attitude to feeding people, chimed with me completely.

Venetian food focuses on fresh ingredients, and a lot of fish. The fish is simply prepared, raw or grilled. Vegetables are fried or only lightly boiled, to retain as much of their own flavour as possible. Meat, though rarely eaten in Venice, is mostly slowly cooked.

Nothing is overdone, and it was this simple approach to food that captured my imagination and gave me the basis for developing the menu at Polpetto. Although I was classically trained in the French style, it didn't take me long to get excited about this type of food.

As time went on, I became more and more interested in ingredients that were slightly off-beat or sometimes forgotten. My approach to cooking relies on a few central ingredients – three at the most, or four at a push. It's become my thing, I guess. I see food in almost filmic terms: a good story always has a single lead, normally with two supporting roles. Any more and the plot becomes confusing and overly elaborate.

Stocking a kitchen is simpler than people think. There are a few key ingredients that no kitchen should be without. They are the building blocks; a kind of backbone to any dish. These shouldn't be overlooked and they all need to be of the highest quality. Olive oil, salt, honey, chocolate, vinegar, flour, eggs, mustard, nuts, unwaxed lemons and lots of fresh herbs are what make simple food shine. None of my food goes without one or more of these ingredients.

I follow the seasons, almost religiously. It is logical that ingredients will always taste better when in season, whether it's white currants, bobby beans, sloe berries, quinces, acorns, coco beans or nettles.

My kitchen is stripped-back and basic, out of necessity, where the Magimix is the only real piece of technology. But this works well, and it's perfect for me.

You have to be creative with what you have. A kitchen can be run on a shoestring but even if you have unlimited resources there should be no waste. Remnant off-cuts of San Daniele ham scraps can be used to season sauces or made into croquettes. Any stale focaccia bread is torn and baked into breadcrumbs, fried into pangrattato or even toasted for bruschetta.

This frugal approach, and a menu that changes sometimes between services, means that the relationship with suppliers is critical. My 'veg man' is brilliant at finding the most obscure and hard-to-obtain items. I receive a text late afternoon to tell me what fish has been caught that very morning. A thick, friendly West Country accent converses with me about supplies of the finest shellfish and seaside vegetables. Even my mum has become a valued supplier, bringing me wild garlic, honeysuckle and nettles from her garden. I'd struggle without them.

Throughout my culinary life I've taken inspiration and sustenance from those early years at Pinewood Cottage. Meals were about making the best of seasonal ingredients, improvising with what we had (even if what we had didn't exactly go together) and experimenting, sometimes to the point of absurdity. But it was fun and it was about sharing, and most of all it was about coming together, being one.

Amongst the pots & pans

With simple food it is particularly important that you buy the best quality ingredients that you can get your hands on.

My kitchen is never without unwaxed lemons, bundles of fresh herbs wrapped in damp cloth and a fine olive oil. I especially like the flavour of Planeta olive oil, which has a clean, slightly bitter beginning and lengthy spiciness at the end.

Punnets of free-range eggs sit on my shelves. I try to buy them from the local farmers' market but otherwise from quality suppliers like Clarence Court, which are easily available in the supermarket.

Using Mulino Marino '00' flour or Polenta Valsugana will get a dish off to a good start. They can be found in any well-stocked Italian deli.

Morcilla, salt cod, Ortiz anchovies and Unio Moscatel vinegar can all be bought at Brindisa or over the internet. They are truly beautiful ingredients to work with and very much valued in my kitchen.

There are three salts I mainly use: Maldon, Cornish and Celtic grey. Maldon and Cornish salt with their flaky pyramid shape work perfectly raw, crushed over a dish to season or in baking. Celtic grey salt is best for salting water and joints of meat. It adds a complexity to food, especially when salt-roasting, which calls for large quantities.

A good pepper mill and black peppercorns are a must. Avoid using anything pre-ground – it just won't have the same freshness.

I often find myself zig-zagging around town gathering all these bits and pieces for my cupboards. Once you have accumulated all these basic ingredients, you will feel ready to tie your apron strings.

The temperatures in my recipes are for fan and gas ovens, as those are what I tend to use. If you have a conventional oven, simply add 20°C to the fan oven temperature. For example, where the recipe says 150°C/gas 3, preheat the oven to 170°C instead.

One final thing: remember to weigh fluids (rather than relying on measuring jugs) wherever possible, especially when preparing bread dough, as it makes for greater accuracy and consistency, which will make all the difference. Converting fluid measurements is simple – just use 1ml:1g for water, stock, alcohol, vinegar, apple juice and milk. Oil is 1ml:0.92g, yoghurt is around 1ml:0.94g and maple syrup 1ml:1.34g.

One

I've always been around olive oil. For me, it's the starting point, the be all and end all. Almost every plate of food I've ever cooked has it in. A drop or two in the pan to begin the cooking process or a trickle over the plate at the very end. Often it's both. And I'm not alone.

People forget how amazing olive oil is because it's become so common. It's almost become invisible and yet it's so essential. More people are using it than ever and global consumption grows every year. In fact it has doubled in the last twenty-five years. What was once considered a rare and valuable commodity has become common or garden.

Olive oil was an early discovery for me because my mum used it for absolutely everything. I come from a big English family but we have always eaten very simply. Every meal was a big spread for everyone to share – a bowl of soup, bread, cold meat, cheese and the ever-present bottle of extra virgin olive oil. With so many mouths to feed this was easier than preparing individual plates. Eating together around a big table meant that everyone talked and we've always been a very close family, I think because of this.

Mum didn't reserve the extra virgin for just mealtimes either. She used to rub it on our sunburn, pour it in our baths, apply it to squeaky doors and stick it in our ears to stave off ear infections. She is an amazing mother but she wasn't a master in the kitchen while I was growing up. She regularly burnt onions in smoking oil when cooking. Of course, I know now why she burnt them – extra virgin olive oil has a much lower smoking point than other oils.

That said, I use olive oil in so many different ways and most recipes don't call for taking it above its smoking point anyway. I use it for almost everything, from sautéing to sweating, from baking bread to searing meat, and for brushing down roasts and fish before cooking. Its varying grades increase its versatility, and the finest should be savoured in its raw state. A dash on a plate of thickly sliced summer-ripe tomatoes; dressing a beef carpaccio; or simply to plunge your bread in.

Think of it as you might salt. Raw olive oil adds body and depth to food, and can balance out acid levels from wine, lemon juice, vinegar and other astringent ingredients. It can also reduce spice levels. Its real genius is that it manages to remain full-bodied without feeling greasy, like most other oils. It's also thicker, and much more aromatic and flavoursome.

We humans are conditioned to crave fats. We love oil-rich dressings on our salads and butter on our bread and potatoes. Fat does equal flavour but olive oil's rich, viscous texture makes dishes tastier by providing an unctuous base to carry those flavours. A bold olive oil is sensational when splashed on a char-grilled steak, for instance. It will emphasise the steak's meatiness and tone down the bitterness of the char.

So there you have it, olive oil is my number one ingredient. Rightfully highly prized for thousands of years.

Best of all, I love it.

Poached rabbit in olive oil with Pink Fir potatoes

This is one of my favourites at Polpetto. It brings back happy memories of early spring days working on new ingredients and ideas. The rabbit needs to marinate for at least six hours, so I prepare it the night before I want to cook it.

Makes four large bowls

For the rabbit:
4 large rabbit legs or
  1 rabbit, jointed
40g salt
½ tbsp caster sugar
4 sprigs of oregano
4 garlic cloves
1 unwaxed lemon
about 500ml extra virgin
  olive oil

For the potatoes:
100g Kalamata olives
500g Pink Fir potatoes
1l chicken stock (or water)
1 unwaxed lemon
3 sprigs of thyme
a pinch of salt
a splash of extra virgin
  olive oil
1 head of celery

Place the rabbit legs on a roasting or baking tray and scatter over the salt, sugar and oregano sprigs. Using the flat of a knife, bash the garlic (still in its skin), then run a peeler over the lemon, cutting slivers of the skin. Fold the bashed garlic and lemon slivers through the salty rabbit legs. Cover with cling film and chill for at least six hours or overnight.

When you are ready to cook, preheat the oven to 150°C/gas 3. Rinse off the marinade and pat the meat dry. Place the rabbit, garlic, lemon and oregano in a deep baking tray. Pour over enough olive oil to cover the meat. Cover the tray securely with foil and place in the preheated oven. Cook gently for three hours. The olive oil needs to be kept just under simmering point, with no bubbles breaking the surface.

Remove the pits from the olives, then roughly chop them to a coarse paste and set aside for later.

After the rabbit legs have been cooking for about two and a half hours, start preparing the potatoes. Pop them whole in a large pan, cover with the chicken stock and place on a high heat. Peel in the lemon rind, then scatter over the thyme sprigs and salt, and add a splash of olive oil. Once the stock has come to the boil, reduce to a gentle simmer for fifteen to twenty minutes until the potatoes are tender. Test that they are cooked by feeling whether a knife goes through easily.

Check the rabbit after three hours – it should be tender, nearly falling off the bone but without much colour. Remove from the oven and set aside while you finish making the broth.

Remove the outer celery sticks and cut long thin ribbons from the pale centre sticks with a peeler. Stir through the potatoes and leave to simmer for a couple of minutes to wilt the celery. Ladle the potato, celery and broth into large bowls and top each with a piece of rabbit, a scattering of olives and some of the oil that the rabbit was cooked in.

Braised lettuce, cockles & bacon

We tend to think of lettuce just as salad, but it can be even better when cooked. Sweet and fragile braised baby gem lettuce works well with cockles and bacon, and new season olive oil is key in bringing these contrasting elements together. It adds a touch of the Mediterranean to what would otherwise be very traditional English fare.

Makes four small bowls

400g cockles (or clams)
4 baby gem lettuce heads
1 onion
1 bunch of spring onions
1l vegetable stock
2 tbsp butter
100g bacon lardons
new season extra virgin
  olive oil, to finish

Prepare the cockles first. Fill the sink with cold water and lower the cockles in. Discard any that are open. Rub them in the cold water with your hands to loosen all the grit, drain through a colander and let the water out of the sink. Repeat this a couple more times to make sure all the grit and dirt has been washed away. If you're not going to use the cockles immediately, keep them in about a centimetre of cold water in a bowl covered with a damp cloth in the fridge.

Cut the baby gems in half and remove the central core. Keeping the leaves still attached, rinse the lettuce halves in cold water. Grate the onion. Chop the spring onions to the thickness of a pound coin.

Pour the vegetable stock into a pan and, as it heats, add the butter, onion and spring onions. Bring the stock to the boil and simmer for a couple of minutes to infuse the onion flavour. Add the lettuce halves and cover with a circle of greaseproof paper topped with a heatproof plate, so that they stay submerged in the stock. Cook for three to four minutes so that they are soft but not sludgy, then remove from the heat.

While the lettuce is cooking, place a large pan (one with a lid) over a low heat, and once it's hot, add the lardons, cooking them relatively slowly so that they go crispy but don't burn. After five to eight minutes the lardons will start to crisp up. Add a ladle of your lettuce stock to the cockles and stir through. Turn up the heat, place the lid on the pan and let the cockles steam for two minutes, then give the pan a shake. The cockles will begin to pop open if they haven't already. Cook for a further couple of minutes then discard any unopened ones. Gently fold the lettuce pieces through the cockles and taste the broth before seasoning as it can be salty.

Ladle some stock and lettuce into each bowl, topple on a couple of spoonfuls of the cockles and lardons, and trickle over the olive oil. Best eaten immediately, with bread to mop up the juices.

Olive oil poached cod with butter lettuce & fennel

This floppy inexpensive lettuce is delicate and sweet, with green curly leaves. Be careful not to overdress it as the delicate soft leaves will go limp. Poaching the cod will stop the fish drying out, and means that it will break into moist plump chunks. This dish also works well with pollock or halibut instead of cod.

Makes two large plates

2 x 170g skinless cod fillets
3 unwaxed lemons
a good pinch of salt
4 sprigs of thyme
about 500ml extra virgin
  olive oil
1 fennel bulb
1 butter lettuce

Preheat the oven to 200°C/gas 7.

Pat the fish dry with kitchen roll and leave on a plate to reach room temperature.

Thinly slice two of the lemons. Season the cod with a good pinch of salt and rub over the flesh. Place in a deep baking tray and layer over the lemon slices and thyme sprigs. Pour over the olive oil – it should cover the fish by about a centimetre, so it's totally submerged. Cover the tray tightly with tin foil and place in the oven for ten to fifteen minutes until the cod is opaque and the flesh flakes easily.

Whilst the cod is cooking, remove the outer layer of the fennel and cut the bulb in half vertically. Using your knife tip, cut the core out leaving the bulb intact so that the remaining leaves stay together. Slice as thinly as possible on a mandolin or by hand. Place the fennel slices in cold water with the juice of half a lemon to keep them crisp and stop any discolouring until serving.

Discard the outer leaves of butter lettuce. Pull the inner leaves back from the heart, rinse under cold water to remove any earth and then tear the leaves into large pieces.

In a bowl, mix the fennel and butter lettuce with a squeeze of juice from the remaining half lemon, warm olive oil from the cod and salt to taste. Strew the fennel and lettuce on the plates, place the fish alongside and serve immediately.

Milk risotto & salmoriglio

This savoury rice pudding is comfort food in the truest sense. It's also easy to prepare and it has an elegance about it. Milk risotto is part of the street food tradition of Florence, while salmoriglio is a Sicilian condiment usually prepared for use with meat or fish. Normally the sauce is made with oregano, parsley and garlic, but I have left these last two out to ensure that it brings a light, floral, herby finish to the rice.

Makes six large bowls

For the risotto:
4 banana shallots
1 garlic clove
1 head of celery
500ml chicken stock
1l milk
100g butter
2 bay leaves
a pinch of salt
300g carnaroli rice
70–80g Pecorino cheese

For the salmoriglio:
8 sprigs of oregano
2 unwaxed lemons
100ml extra virgin olive oil
salt

Peel the shallots and garlic clove. Bash the garlic with the flat of your knife and chop through the squashed clove (I add a pinch of salt to help to break it down). Finely dice the banana shallots and set aside. Discarding the outer celery stalks, pick the leaves and keep them to garnish. Finely dice the paler centre stalks and set aside.

Pour the stock into a pan and put it on a back burner over a low heat to warm up. Do the same with the milk in a separate pan.

In another pan melt two thirds of the butter over a low heat, then add the shallots, garlic, celery, bay leaves and salt. Cover and leave to sweat down, checking after ten minutes – the vegetables should be soft and tender without colour.

Pour in the rice, turn up the heat and give the contents a good stir to coat each grain of rice in the buttery mixture. Keep stirring it for a couple of minutes until the rice becomes translucent. Add a ladle of stock at a time, stirring until the liquid is absorbed before adding the next one. Then add the milk in the same way.

While the rice is cooking, grate the Pecorino and make the salmoriglio. Pick the leaves from the oregano and zest the lemons. Roughly chop the zest and oregano together, trying not to bruise the oregano leaves, then place in a small bowl and stir in the olive oil along with a good squeeze of lemon juice and salt to taste (I add a good pinch).

Remove the risotto from the heat and stir through the Pecorino and the remaining butter. Eat from shallow bowls with a little of the salmoriglio over the top.

Bruschetta

This is the best way to use up stale bread. It's also an excellent way to taste a good quality olive oil. This works particularly well with sourdough or ciabatta, but whatever bread you use, make sure it is stale as it needs to be quite hard once toasted so that you can grate the garlic on it.

Makes two slices

Grill the bread until it's crisp.

2 thin slices of stale bread
1 garlic clove
extra virgin olive oil

Peel the garlic and rub the toasted bread with it. You need effectively to grate the garlic onto the bread, ensuring that there are no lumps so that there is a smooth finish when you're done.

Dribble over your favourite olive oil and serve straight away.

Drowned tomatoes

As suggested, these tomatoes are swimming, or even drowned, in olive oil, which accentuates their sweetness and depth. Especially pleasing through crisp salad leaves, toppled over a soft poached egg on toast or even steamed with clams. You can use any variety of tomato to make this recipe, from golden cherry to sweet baby plum, but I find that heritage work particularly well.

Serves four to six

550g mixed heritage tomatoes
4 garlic cloves
1 bunch of thyme
2 or 3 bay leaves
1 tsp sugar
a pinch of salt
about 250ml extra virgin
*   olive oil*

Preheat the oven to 170°C/gas 5.

Run the tomatoes under cold water and pick out any stalks.

Place the garlic cloves in warm water for a couple of minutes – this helps to loosen the skin. Pop them out of their skins.

Slice the tomatoes in half and gently lodge them cut-side down in a pan or casserole dish that can go in the oven. Thinly slice the garlic and scatter it over the tomatoes. Drop over the thyme and bay leaves, and sprinkle with the sugar and salt. Pour over the olive oil until the tomatoes are sitting in about half a centimetre of it.

Bake for about forty-five minutes until the tomatoes are soft, a little wrinkly and blistered and have absorbed most of the olive oil.

These will keep for a few days in a jar or airtight container stored in a cool place or, if cooled first and kept under a layer of olive oil, up to a week in the fridge.

Tapenade

This French classic is beautifully moreish. You can make it by hand or in a food processor. In either case, I think the texture is a personal thing. I prefer a coarse mixture but some people prefer it smoother and runnier, so add the olive oil to taste. The olives taste best if you buy them cured in olive oil as it retains their freshness and olivey flavour. I often squeeze this tapenade under the skin of a chicken before slow roasting it, and it's perfect on toasted bread as an afternoon nibble.

Makes 500g

1 garlic clove
1 fresh red chilli, whole
2 tbsp capers
3 anchovy fillets
250g green olives, pitted
150g Kalamata olives, pitted
a pinch of dried oregano
1 small handful of
   flat-leaf parsley
4 sprigs of thyme
1 unwaxed lemon
125ml extra virgin olive oil,
   plus extra

Peel the garlic and roughly chop the chilli. Rinse the capers under cold running water.

Grind the garlic to a fine paste using a mortar and pestle. Add the chilli pieces, capers, anchovies, olives and oregano to the garlic and pound together until they form a coarse paste.

Pick the parsley and thyme leaves, roughly chop and stir through the olive paste. Zest over the lemon, then halve and squeeze in the juice. Trickle in the olive oil and stir – if necessary add more oil until it combines to your preferred texture.

Alternatively put everything in a food processor and blend together.

Mayonnaise

Most mayonnaises are made with ordinary flavourless oils, such as sunflower. I always make mine with a combination of extra virgin olive oil and rapeseed. I love the fruity flavour that the olives give to extra virgin oil, balanced by the lightly-flavoured rapeseed oil. There is something so satisfying about making your own mayonnaise, and there's nothing like fresh mayonnaise on salads, vegetables and crusty bread.

Enough for eight to ten heaped tablespoonfuls

3 medium egg yolks
a pinch of salt
2 heaped tsp English mustard
100ml rapeseed oil
about 200ml extra virgin olive oil
juice of 1 unwaxed lemon

Put the yolks in a large bowl with a pinch of salt. Add the mustard and whisk. Slowly trickle in the rapeseed oil, whisking continuously, and then do the same with the olive oil. The whisk will begin to feel heavier and the mixture will begin to look thick and wobbly. When you get to this point be careful because you may not need to use all the oil. If the mixture gets too thick or becomes shiny and looks as if it is about to split you can add a splash of lukewarm water to loosen it.

Slowly add the lemon juice to taste – this will cause the mixture to turn whiter and more mayonnaise-y. Stir through salt and pepper to taste, along with another splash of lukewarm water if it seems too thick.

Fresh mayonnaise should be stored in a jar or airtight container in the fridge and eaten within a day or two at the most.

Sauces & dressings

Dill, caper & lemon

My favourite way to have this sauce is with a whole grilled sea bream or similar white fish.

1 bunch of dill
½ tbsp Lilliput capers
zest of 1 unwaxed lemon
100ml extra virgin olive oil
a pinch of salt

Chop the dill roughly and place in a bowl. Do the same with the capers. Zest in the lemon. Pour in the olive oil with a pinch of salt and stir together. Any you don't use will keep for a couple of days if stored in a jar or airtight container in the fridge, although the vibrant green colour of the freshly-made dressing will fade.

Rosemary & anchovy

This simple dressing works really well with cauliflower and roasted pine nuts, broccoli or lamb. I particularly like using Ortiz tinned anchovy fillets for this.

1 sprig of rosemary
4 anchovy fillets
1 unwaxed lemon
50ml extra virgin olive oil
salt and black pepper

Roughly chop the rosemary and pound it with the anchovy fillets using a mortar and pestle until they become a rough, chunky paste. Zest in the lemon, then halve it and squeeze in a little juice. Pour in the olive oil and stir through salt and pepper to taste. Any left over can be stored for up to a couple of days in a jar or airtight container in the fridge.

Classic olive oil dressing

For me, this is the simplest and best way to dress leaves or other food.

3–4 tbsp extra virgin olive oil
juice of 1 unwaxed lemon
salt

Make by whisking the olive oil with lemon juice, then add salt to taste.

Marinades

I marinade almost every piece of meat I cook. This technique adds depth of flavour and can add days to the normal shelf life of uncooked meat. It's also a great way to introduce new flavours: try using oregano, fennel or caraway seeds – whatever inspires you.

For lamb or beef

Enough for a big joint

1 head of garlic
2 shallots
2 tsp honey
500ml extra virgin olive oil
3 sprigs of rosemary
1 tsp pink peppercorns

Cut the garlic head and peeled shallots in half. Mix the honey and oil together with a whisk in a large bowl and then stir in the other ingredients. Submerge the meat in it. Cover the bowl securely (or place the meat and marinade in an airtight container) and leave in the fridge for at least a couple of hours or overnight.

For chicken or rabbit

Enough for a whole chicken or rabbit

1 unwaxed lemon
1 head of garlic
3 sprigs of oregano
500ml extra virgin olive oil

Shave the peel from the lemon. Cut the garlic head in half horizontally. Mix the lemon shavings, garlic head and other ingredients together in a large bowl. Put the meat in the bowl and smear with the marinade, then cover securely and leave in the fridge for at least a couple of hours or overnight.

For feta or goat's cheese

Enough for 250g cheese

1 garlic clove
3 sprigs of thyme
3 black peppercorns
a pinch of dried chilli flakes
200ml extra virgin olive oil

Peel and finely slice the garlic. Mix the garlic and other ingredients together in a bowl, jar or airtight container, stir in the cheese, cover tightly and marinade for at least twenty-four hours until all the flavours are infused. This will keep for up to a week if stored in the fridge.

Focaccia

I eat focaccia all the time. This type of flat oven-baked bread has been made in Italy since Roman times when it was cooked in the ashes of the fireplace and its name comes from the Latin word for hearth. My sous chef, Libby Greenfield, brought this recipe with her when she started. Focaccia is especially oily. It can seem quite odd to make the dough so wet, but it gives the bread such richness that it's hard to stop eating. For best results I prepare the dough the day before and leave the sticky mixture to rise and grow bubbles overnight before baking.

Makes one large loaf
(roughly A4 size)

Dough:
200g potatoes
600g '00' flour, plus extra
100g strong flour
17g fresh yeast
500ml lukewarm water
60ml extra virgin olive oil
22g salt

To top:
50ml lukewarm water
125ml extra virgin olive oil
flaky sea salt

Peel and evenly dice the potatoes. Place in a pan of cold salted water, bring to the boil and cook for ten minutes or until very soft. Drain and mash them through a fine sieve or ricer while still warm.

In a large bowl combine the flours and the mashed potato, rubbing through with your fingers to ensure there are no lumps.

Mix the yeast and a small amount of the warm water in a large jug and leave it for a few minutes to dissolve completely. Then add the remaining water and the oil, whisking to combine.

Make a well in the flour-potato mixture and add the yeasty liquid along with the salt. Bring the mixture together with your hands and work it in the bowl (or with a dough hook in a mixer) until totally combined. The dough is meant to be runny and a little lumpy – don't panic.

Cover the bowl loosely with cling film and leave in the fridge overnight, making sure the bowl is big enough for the dough to expand considerably (it can nearly triple in size). Give the dough a smack on top to knock it back if it is getting too big and threatens to overflow the bowl.

Thirty minutes or so before you want to bake, take the bowl out of the fridge and allow the dough to come to room temperature. Once the dough has expanded to the edge of the bowl and is covered with lots of air bubbles, it is ready.

Lightly flour the work surface, then use a bread paddle or dough scraper to turn the dough out onto it. The dough will be very soft. Ease and stretch it into a large rectangle (about A4 size) using your fingertips, taking care not to lose all the air in the dough. Then dust gently with flour and place on the baking tray. Cover loosely with a clean tea towel and leave in a warm place to prove for one hour or until it has doubled in size.

Preheat the oven to 220°C/gas 9. Prepare a large baking tray with a thin layer of olive oil.

In a large jug, whisk together the warm water and olive oil to pour on top.

Use your fingers to make indentations in the top of the dough, then pour over your water-olive oil mixture and sprinkle with a little sea salt. Bake for ten minutes at the very high heat then turn the oven down to 190°C/gas 7 and bake for a further thirty minutes until the focaccia has risen and is evenly browned.

Turn out upside-down on a rack and leave to cool, if you can wait that long.

Pistachio, cardamom and olive oil cake

Moist, fragrant and very green. It's perfect with a dollop of loosely whipped cream and maybe a sprinkle of icing sugar.

Serves eight

200g shelled pistachios
8 cardamom pods
100g quick-cook polenta
1 tsp baking powder
50g butter
175ml extra virgin olive oil
3 medium eggs,
  at room temperature
200g caster sugar
1 unwaxed lemon

Preheat the oven to 170°C/gas 5. Grease and line a 23cm round deep baking tin.

Place the pistachios on a dry baking tray and toast in the oven for three minutes until they have a greasy shine and nutty aroma. Remove and set aside to cool.

Bash the cardamom pods using a pestle and mortar, discard the husks, and grind the seeds to a fine powder.

Tip the pistachios and cardamom powder into a food processor and pulse until they're finely ground. Pour the pistachios into a large bowl with the polenta and baking powder and mix until evenly combined.

Place the butter and olive oil in a small pan on a low heat until the butter has melted but not boiled. Leave to cool slightly.

In a second large bowl, whisk the eggs and sugar together until light, fluffy and thick enough to hold a ribbon on the surface of the mixture. Very slowly trickle in the butter and oil, slowly whisking it into the eggs until fully incorporated, then gently fold through the nut and polenta mixture. Zest over the lemon, then halve and add the juice as well. Stir to combine.

Pour into the greased tin and bake for forty-five to fifty minutes. Check that a skewer comes out clean and the surface springs back a little when you press in the centre. The cake will have risen with a golden top, but don't be upset if the middle has collapsed slightly or even cracked.

Rest in the tin until cool, and serve in thick slices with a dollop of cream. This cake is so moist that it actually improves in flavour if kept for a day or two. However, I like to serve it on the day of baking before its vibrant green colour starts to fade.

Olive oil & brown sugar ice cream

It might seem an odd combination, but actually olive oil brings a velvety richness to ice cream while keeping it light with its slightly green, heady fragrance.

Serves four
  (makes about 800ml)

250ml double cream
330ml whole milk
80g Muscovado sugar
5 medium egg yolks
125ml fruity extra virgin
  olive oil
a pinch of salt

Pour the cream and milk into a heavy-bottomed pan and bring to the boil then remove from the heat. Meanwhile whisk the sugar and egg yolks together until pale and fluffy. Stream the warm cream and milk into the sugar and egg yolks, stirring to combine.

Pass the mixture through a fine sieve into a clean pan and place it on a low heat, stirring continuously to keep the eggs from scrambling. When the mixture has thickened slightly and evenly coats the back of a spoon, pass it through a fine sieve again into a clean bowl and allow to cool to room temperature.

Once it's at room temperature, stir through the olive oil and salt. Churn in an ice cream machine. Alternatively, pour it into a shallow tray and freeze for thirty minutes, then take it out and whisk through before returning it to the freezer. Whisk and refreeze three or four times until smooth and set.

I find that homemade ice cream is best eaten within a couple of days of making it, but it will keep in the freezer for a couple of months.

Tipsy greengage cake

When you work in a busy restaurant kitchen you often don't have the time to notice the seasons outside, but certain fruits mark the change from one season to the next, and for me the beautiful greengage always symbolises the beginning of autumn. The grassy-green olive oil helps to offset the sweetness of the fruit, Marsala wine and honey. This recipe works equally well with other autumn fruits such as plums or figs. The drunken fruit can be stored in a jar in a cool place for a week or two.

Serves eight

8 under-ripe greengages
300ml Marsala wine
1 tbsp honey
½ tsp almond essence
6 medium eggs,
    at room temperature
100ml extra virgin olive oil
120g butter,
    at room temperature
120g caster sugar
120g dark brown sugar
130g quick-cook polenta
140g plain flour
2 tsp baking powder
a pinch of salt
zest of 1 unwaxed lemon
1 tbsp Demerara sugar

Rinse the greengages under cold running water and pat dry. Using a cocktail stick, pierce the fruit a few times so that the greengages will be able to absorb the wine properly. Place the fruit in a heat-proof container with a good seal, like a Kilner jar.

Pour the Marsala, honey and almond essence into a saucepan and bring it to a gentle simmer. Once the honey is dissolved, bring the syrupy mixture to the boil for a couple of minutes. Remove it from the heat and allow to cool a little. Then pour the syrup over the greengages, seal the jar and leave it overnight.

Preheat the oven to 180°C/gas 6. Grease and line a 23cm round deep baking tin.

In a large bowl whisk together the eggs and olive oil until pale and fluffy. In a separate bowl, beat the butter, caster sugar and dark brown sugar together until also nice and fluffy. Slowly dribble in the oil-egg mixture. Fold through all the dry ingredients and lemon zest.

Remove the greengages from the jar, halve them and remove their stones.

Pour the batter into the cake tin and loosely scatter the halved greengages over the top. Bake in the oven for thirty minutes then sprinkle on the Demerara. Reduce the temperature to 160°C/gas 4 and bake for twenty minutes until golden and firm.

Remove from the oven and spoon over some of the Marsala syrup while the cake is still hot, then leave to cool in the tin. Any leftover syrup will keep for up to a month in the fridge. Serve this cake in generous wedges with spoonfuls of cream.

Olive oil, chocolate & orange cake

Every year at Christmas my brother would crack the Terry's chocolate orange on my head, but apart from this I've always been rather partial to the combination of chocolate and orange. Olive oil does a great job in keeping this cake moist and it helps to bring out the fruity orange flavour. This is a great afternoon tea pick-me-up and reminds me of a giant moist Jaffa cake.

Serves eight

3 medium oranges
260g blanched almonds
6 medium eggs,
   at room temperature
400g golden caster sugar
6 tbsp extra virgin olive oil
260g plain flour
1 tbsp baking powder
1½ tsp bicarbonate of soda
a good pinch of salt

For the filling and topping:
150g dark chocolate
115g butter
150g Muscovado sugar
200ml double cream
a large pinch of flaky sea salt

Grease and line three 23cm round baking tins and preheat the oven to 180°C/gas 6.

Place the whole, lightly scrubbed oranges in a large pan and cover with water. Bring it to the boil then leave to simmer gently for an hour. While the oranges are simmering, toast the almonds for about three minutes on a dry baking tray, until they give off a nice nutty aroma. Let the almonds cool. Grind them to a fine consistency in a food processor and set aside.

After an hour's simmering, remove the oranges from the pan and let them cool slightly.

Once the oranges are cool enough to handle, tear them open and remove the pips and any stalks. Place in a food processor and blitz to a smooth paste. Scoop the orange paste into a bowl, stir the almonds into it and set aside.

In a large bowl whisk the eggs with the sugar until pale and fluffy. Slowly trickle in the olive oil, whisking as you go. Gently fold through the flour, raising agents and salt, followed by the orange and almond paste, folding until evenly combined.

Pour the cake mixture into the prepared tins and bake at 180°C/ gas 6 for twenty to twenty-five minutes, or until a skewer poked into the centre comes out clean. While the cakes are baking, make the topping.

Break up the dark chocolate, cut up the butter and drop them into a heatproof bowl placed over a pan of simmering water, stirring every so often to help them to melt together. Once the butter and chocolate have melted and combined, remove the bowl from the heat and set aside.

Pour the sugar and cream in a pan and place on a low heat, stirring occasionally. Once the sugar is dissolved, turn up the heat and bring to the boil (making sure not to do what I always do and let the cream boil over – if it does, take it off the heat immediately and blow on it until it simmers down!). Then lower the heat and simmer for about five minutes to reduce the sugary-cream mixture; it bubbles like a witch's cauldron so be careful.

Remove from the heat and stir through the chocolate and butter. Leave the mixture to cool, stirring it from time to time to make sure that it doesn't set.

By now the cake layers should have finished baking. Whilst you wait for the chocolate mixture to cool down, carefully remove the cakes from the tins and let them cool completely on a wire rack.

After about ten to fifteen minutes' cooling, the topping should be thick and glossy. Put half of it on one cake layer and split the rest between the other two. Spread the topping over each layer, working from the centre outwards. Pile the layers on top of each other, with the thickest layer of chocolate as the top of the cake. Finally, sprinkle over a generous pinch of flaky salt. Cut into slices and eat just as it is at teatime, or serve as a dessert with a little crème fraiche.

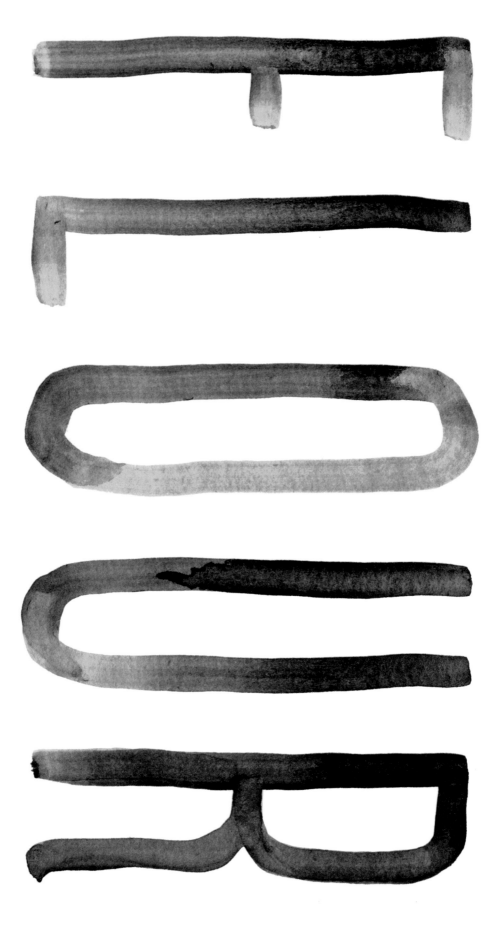

Two

You may think it mundane, a bit dull even, but flour is central to many recipes, and it is one of the most valuable ingredients in any kitchen. Flour is the backbone of so much – pastry, pasta, sauces, brioche, sticky buns, cakes, pancakes, sourdough, roux… It binds other ingredients together and provides a base for almost every style of cooking. Flour is a beautiful word too, coming from the French word 'fleur', meaning blossom or flower.

Above all I simply love bread and I could never imagine it not being part of my day. As a child my mother would buy it freshly baked from our local farm shop and a mouse-like hole would appear at the bottom of the loaf even before Mum had paid; I just couldn't resist it. When asked, I would blame my brothers and sisters with a naughty glint, and she would smile and shake her head. One of my favourite memories is making hedgehogs out of bread dough with my little sister, using scissors to cut spikes and sticking on sultanas as eyes.

Flour was as much part of my playtimes as my meal times. I remember the excitement at weekends when we'd break open a can of Pillsbury dough, roll it out and lay a finger of chocolate across it before folding it up to bake our very own croissants or pain au chocolat for the morning breakfast.

In my early days in the kitchen I learnt many little tricks that I've found so useful throughout my career. Silly as it sounds, the most important tip for any baker is to ensure that you always measure your flour correctly. If you add too much your baking will become dry and dense, which is why homemade bread is often like a brick. Don't panic and add lots more flour when kneading, even if the dough looks like sloppy porridge at first, as it will come together with some elbow grease.

Time is the key. It makes a real difference between a good, bad or ugly loaf. I like to leave the dough overnight in the fridge. Your bread will have a better rise and complexity of taste that's well worth the wait.

Flour, yeast, water and salt are all you really need. No fancy equipment will do it better than your hands, but a dough scraper helps. I find it very useful. If you can't find one you can simply cut a small rectangle out of a plastic lid.

I started my career working as a pastry chef in Yorkshire. It was really tough: I worked seven days a week for a month and never earned a penny, but I was learning the basics. Work started at 10pm and finished sixteen hours later. I was making breads using traditional techniques with natural ingredients entirely by hand and baking many different loaves off at sunrise. I remember carrying 25kg bags of flour – more than half my bodyweight – and kneading 10kg of wet sticky dough first thing in the morning. This is the best kind of tactile cooking, when you really get a feel for the substance you are preparing.

That summer I set up my very own stall with stacks of different shaped loaves, sticky buns and cakes. My foolproof sponge is to just weigh four eggs in their shells for the exact measurement of flour (as well as butter and sugar as it happens) along with a dash of milk.

Far too often, people are daunted by making their own pastry. All it needs is a light touch and to be chilled before you handle it. Not only does chilling make the pastry easier to work, it also improves the flavour considerably.

I have learned that working with flour is a slow process. It takes time and patience, effort and precision but there's a feeling of craftsmanship and a real sense of satisfaction when you make something by hand from scratch, something that has taken time and love to prepare.

Bakeries have always fascinated me – the smell of freshly baked bread, the warmth, the sense that someone has created something wonderful from a simple bag of flour. Wherever I go in the world, the first thing I do is look for a bakery. They hold innumerable towns and villages together, serving people from all walks of life who are hungry for a humble loaf or simple tea cake. It's such a pity that so many bakeries in England have gone to the wall now and that so few of our children will ever know the smell of freshly baked bread in the morning air.

Nettle gnudi

Gnudi means 'nude' in Italian and is a stripped-back gnocchi. Whipping the ricotta makes these into light pillows rather than heavy gnocchi-like lumps, and the nettles work well for both texture and taste – like hairy spinach. Nettles start sprouting up as early as February and continue right through the spring and summer. They are best eaten in the spring while still young and tender, and usually appear in the same places year after year which makes them easy to find. Fortunately they lose their sting when cooked but be careful when you are preparing them. If you find nettles too daunting, you can simply exchange them for young tender spinach leaves, but nettles really are worth the trouble. These gnudi are very rich so serve six or seven per person.

Makes six small plates

300g freshly picked nettles
500g ricotta
a trickle of extra virgin olive oil
½ nutmeg
zest of 1 unwaxed lemon
100g Parmesan
1kg semolina flour
100g walnuts
1 tbsp butter
16 thin slices of lardo

Pick through the nettles using tongs and rubber gloves as they will still sting at this point. Discard the tough stalks, then wash the nettles thoroughly, still using gloves and tongs. With the water still clinging onto the leaves, throw them into a large pan over a low heat, add a pinch of salt and pop a lid on. Wilt the nettles down for a few minutes in the same way as you would spinach, then drain in a colander over a bowl, reserving the green liquid. Leave the nettles and reserved liquid to cool.

Wrap the ricotta in a clean tea towel or muslin and, pressing it into a sieve, squeeze out as much liquid as you can and discard.

When the nettles are cool enough to handle, squeeze them into a sieve over the bowl containing the reserved green liquid to extract as much water as possible. Finely chop the nettles and set aside.

Tip the ricotta into a large bowl and whisk until it becomes firm – almost dough-like – and the whisk feels heavy. This should take about eight minutes.

Trickle in a little olive oil, grate over the nutmeg and lemon zest, and season with salt and black pepper. Give the sticky mixture a good stir then finely grate in the Parmesan and add the nettles, stirring well to bring all the ingredients together. Press the mixture into a shallow tray and chill uncovered in the fridge for at least one hour (preferably two hours for best results).

Take the ricotta mixture out of the fridge. Fill another shallow tray with the semolina flour. Take a large pinch of the mixture and roll into a mini marshmallow shape between your fingers, squaring off the ends. Drop into the semolina flour and bury it. Repeat this process until all the mixture is finished, then give the semolina tray a good shake so that all the pieces are completely submerged. Place in the fridge overnight (or for at least a couple of hours) while the moisture in the mixture bonds with the semolina coating.

About thirty minutes before you want to serve, preheat the oven to 180°C/gas 6. Toast the walnuts on a dry baking tray for a couple of minutes. Let them cool then roughly chop them.

Bring a large pan of salted water to the boil. Fish the gnudi out of the semolina and cook in the salted water until they bob up to the surface – this should take about two minutes.

While the gnudi are cooking, melt the butter in a large pan until it begins to foam and bubble. Using a slotted spoon, drain the gnudi and drop them into the butter along with a scant tablespoonful of the cooking liquor. Swirl them about gently over a low heat, taking care not to break them up.

Spoon the gnudi and sauce onto warm plates, drape over the lardo and sprinkle with the chopped walnuts. Finally drizzle over some more extra virgin olive oil. Serve immediately.

Panzanella

Old bread doesn't need to be thrown away. Slightly stale bread is perfect for this rustic Tuscan salad – just make sure the bread's only stale, not mouldy! Pick the ripest tomatoes you can get your hands on and always keep them at room temperature. This will make all the difference to their flavour.

Makes 4 small plates

100g stale bread
extra virgin olive oil
a large pinch of salt
½ red onion
500g ripe tomatoes
about 4–6 basil leaves
4 tbsp Moscatel or red
   wine vinegar
a pinch of sugar

Preheat the oven to 150°C/gas 3.

Tear the bread into largish pieces and place them on a baking tray. Generously drizzle over some olive oil, sprinkle with salt and place in the oven until golden and crisp – this should take five to eight minutes.

While the bread is in the oven, finely slice the red onion into half-moons. Place the chopped onion in a bowl, cover with cold water and leave for three minutes – this will help to remove the overly strong onion flavour, so as not to overpower the tomatoes. Drain and set aside.

Remove the tomato stalks then chop, halve or quarter the tomatoes randomly to provide texture. Scoop the tomatoes into a large shallow bowl, then toss through the onion, bread and roughly torn basil leaves. Pour over the vinegar and three tablespoons of olive oil, sprinkle with the sugar and season with salt and black pepper. Fold the tomatoes and bread through the oil and vinegar, pressing the bread into the juices.

Leave the mixture in the bowl to steep for ten minutes then spoon out onto plates to serve.

Roasted grey-legged partridge & bread sauce

A spoonful of bread sauce is one of the most comforting things. I tend to infuse the milk a day before I want to make the sauce, as the flavour just improves more and more – I just warm it when I want to make the sauce. When I think of bread sauce I think of roasts, and you can't beat roast partridge with its delicate flesh. The native grey-legged partridge is far superior to the red-legged non-native variety. Partridge is a small bird, so serve one per person.

Makes two large plates

2 garlic cloves
2 grey-legged partridges
6 sprigs of thyme
2 tsp extra virgin olive oil
2 pinches of salt
2 pinches of black pepper
1 tbsp butter

For the sauce:
1 clove
½ onion, peeled
1 bay leaf
2 sprigs of thyme
4 peppercorns
2 tbsp double cream
1 tsp butter
200ml milk
65g stale sourdough bread
fresh nutmeg, finely grated

Heat the oven to 180°C/gas 6.

Start by making the sauce. Gently pierce the clove into the flesh of the half onion. Place the clove-studded onion half, bay leaf, thyme sprigs, peppercorns, cream, butter and milk in a medium-sized heavy-bottomed pan and bring to a gentle simmer. Allow to simmer very gently while the milk infuses for twenty to twenty-five minutes or so, until the meat comes out of the oven.

While the milk is infusing away, bash the garlic cloves. Rub each bird with one bashed garlic clove, half the thyme, a teaspoon of olive oil and a pinch of salt and pepper. Then stick a bashed garlic clove, thyme sprigs and the butter (divided between the two) into the cavity of each bird.

Heat a large pan until it is close to smoking point then put in the partridges breast-side down and fry until golden (three to five minutes). Transfer the birds to a roasting tray and pop in the oven for ten to fifteen minutes until the flesh feels firm to the touch. Remove from the oven, wrap in foil and let the meat rest for ten minutes.

While the meat is resting, pulse the bread (crusts on) to a coarse crumb in a blender then tip into a small bowl. Remove the saucepan from the heat and immediately strain the milk over the crumbs. Stir the hot mixture until it combines, then grate over the nutmeg and season with a good pinch of salt and cracked black pepper.

Snip each partridge into four joints with scissors so that you have two breast portions and two leg portions, or simply serve whole. Place the partridges on plates and pour over any cooking juices before spooning over the bread sauce and serving straight away with steamed greens, ideally kale or cavalo nero.

Chestnut maltagliati, sage & butter

Maltagliati means 'badly cut' in Italian and was traditionally a great way to use up scraps of pasta discarded when making other shapes. Here I deliberately cut the pasta sheets randomly into different shapes. I like the fact that imperfections are celebrated and delicious. It's not serious or hard work, just a lot of enjoyment. Any pasta that you don't cook straight away can be dusted with semolina and left on a tray in a warm place until completely dry, then stored in an airtight container for a couple of weeks.

Makes four to six large plates

250g chestnut flour
250g '00' flour
4 medium eggs
3 medium egg yolks
semolina flour, for dusting
200g skinned chestnuts
1 tsp dried chilli
zest of 1 unwaxed lemon
8 sage leaves
2 tbsp butter
about 100g Parmesan
extra virgin olive oil

Tip the chestnut and '00' flours into a mixer and pulse until they're well blended together. Trickle in the whole eggs and yolks and pulse again until the mixture comes together and forms a ball. Alternatively sift the two flours into a large bowl, make a well in the middle, add the eggs and yolks and use your fingers to bring it all together.

Place the dough on a surface that has been lightly dusted with semolina flour and knead until you have a smooth ball. Dust the dough with semolina flour, wrap tightly in cling film and chill for a few hours or overnight.

Liberally sprinkle some more semolina flour on the work surface, a rolling pin and a large baking tray. Roll out the dough until it's about the thickness of a penny and almost transparent. Roughly cut into any old shapes, but make sure they are of roughly similar sizes so that the pasta will cook evenly. Lay the cut shapes on the baking tray, dust with semolina flour and set aside somewhere warm for an hour or two (or overnight) until they are dry.

While the pasta is drying, use your hands to crumble the chestnuts into a bowl, add the dried chilli and lemon zest and give the bowl a shake to combine.

Pick the sage leaves and set aside.

When the pasta has dried, put a large pan of salted water on to boil. While the water is heating up, dust the excess semolina from the pasta shapes. Place another pan on the lowest heat, dollop in the butter and add the sage, keeping an eye on it as it heats to make sure it doesn't burn.

When the water is boiling, tip in the pasta and cook for two minutes until 'al dente'. Use a slotted spoon to drain the pasta, reserving some of the cooking water.

Scatter the chilli-lemon chestnuts into the melted butter, grate in a little Parmesan (three good passes over the grater should do it) and then fold the pasta through it. If the sauce looks too thick, add a couple of spoonfuls of the pasta cooking water to loosen it. Reduce the sauce for a minute or so to intensify the flavours.

Serve with a trickle of olive oil and a sprinkle of Parmesan.

Walnut & caraway bread

There is nothing quite like the smell of freshly baked bread. It has the Pied Piper effect in any kitchen, and is always best eaten simply, smeared in butter or dipped in olive oil.

Makes two small loaves or one large one

Preheat the oven to 180°C/gas 6. Lightly oil one baking tray and lightly flour another.

For the nuts and seeds:
300g walnuts
2 tbsp caraway seeds
a pinch of salt
1½ tbsp honey
1 tbsp butter, at room temperature

Toast the walnuts and caraway seeds with a pinch of salt on the lightly-oiled baking tray for three minutes until you start to smell the nutty fragrant aromas release and the nuts turn golden brown. Remove from the oven and set aside to cool slightly.

Spoon the honey, butter and half the walnut-seed mixture into a blender (or use a mortar and pestle) and grind to a fine paste.

For the dough:
400g strong flour, plus extra
100g rye flour
10g salt
10g fresh yeast
300ml lukewarm water
1 handful of polenta (cornmeal)

Mix the flours in a large bowl and bury the salt to the side. Crumble the yeast into the flour between your fingers and mix through. Scoop in the honey paste and pour in the water. Combine as evenly as you can with your fingertips – the dough will be very sticky but don't panic. Then work the dough with your hands and a plastic scraper if you have one, lifting the dough up and folding it over itself to trap air and work the gluten.

Once the dough is fully combined with no floury lumps, turn it onto a clean work surface. Use your hands like shovels to grab the dough from underneath, lifting it up, stretching it and then flipping and folding the mixture over onto itself. Keep repeating this until it starts to come together into a ball (or simply let a mixer with a dough hook do all the work for you, mixing for ten minutes).

Work in the other half of the walnut-seed mixture until evenly spread throughout, then shape the dough into a ball. Save on washing up and lightly dust the same bowl plus the dough and a clean tea towel with flour. Place the dough in the bowl, covered with the tea towel, and leave in a warm place for an hour to rise.

Scrape and scoop the risen dough onto a lightly floured surface, shape it into a ball (or divide in two and shape each half into a ball, if you prefer to make two small loaves) and place on the lightly floured tray.

Cover again with the tea towel and leave in a warm place for another hour to prove.

Preheat the oven to 220°C/gas 9.

Poke a finger into the side of the ballooned dough: it's ready when your fingerprint immediately bounces back. Dust the top with the polenta then slash a shallow criss-cross pattern into the top of the dough and place in the hot oven, with a splash of cold water on the floor of the oven to help create steam. Bake at the high heat for ten minutes, then reduce the heat to 200°C/gas 7 and bake for a further twenty minutes (or ten minutes, if you are making two small loaves).

Lift the bread out of the oven and cool on a wire rack to avoid a soggy bottom. This bread is particularly good smeared with a salty butter or Montgomery's Cheddar. It's best eaten moments after being baked, but will keep for a couple of days for toast.

Steamed apple & treacle pudding

The quintessential British dessert – steaming hot and syrupy sweet.
Nobody does it better. Not even the Italians.

Serves four to six

3 apples
3 tbsp golden syrup
140g butter, at room
*   temperature*
125g caster sugar
zest of 2 unwaxed lemons
2 medium eggs,
*   at room temperature*
125g plain flour
2 tsp baking powder
2 tbsp milk

Butter and lightly flour a 1.2 litre pudding basin.

Peel, core and roughly chop the apples into small pieces. Melt the golden syrup with a tablespoon of the butter in a saucepan on a low heat. Cook for a couple of minutes until the buttery syrup begins to froth and bubble, then fold through the apple and cook for another five minutes.

In a large bowl beat together the rest of the butter, the sugar and the lemon zest until pale and fluffy. In a separate bowl loosely beat the eggs. Slowly trickle the eggs into the butter and sugar mixture, beating all the while. Fold through the flour and baking powder, then fold through the milk until the batter reaches a dropping consistency.

Pour the syrupy apple mixture into the greased basin, then spoon over the batter.

Cut two squares of greaseproof paper and one of foil, each large enough to overlap the edges of the basin by about four centimetres. Layer the squares, greaseproof first then foil on top, and fold into a pleat across the centre. Place on top of the basin with the pleat across the middle, and fasten tightly with a rubber band or string.

Half-fill a large, deep pan with water and place an upturned heatproof plate at the bottom. Place the pan on the stove and when the water is simmering, lower the wrapped pudding onto the centre of the plate. Cover the pan with a tight fitting lid and steam the pudding on a medium heat for one hour and fifteen minutes, or until a skewer poked into the centre comes out clean. Check on it as it cooks, topping up the water if need be. If you use the skewer test to check and it's not quite ready, make sure you reseal the top, covering the hole before continuing to cook; otherwise the sponge will become soggy from the steam.

Remove the pudding carefully from the pan and leave to stand for at least ten minutes before unwrapping and turning out onto a warmed plate. Best served with custard (page 227) or cream.

Sweet pastry

The first time I tried making this it was an unmitigated disaster but it's worth persevering even if you too find it tricky to begin with. I like my pastry extra buttery with a crumbly short texture, which means you have to move extra quickly when lining the tin because otherwise it falls apart. In my opinion, homemade pastry is always superior to the kind you buy in the shops. I've even been known to eat it raw!

Makes enough to line a 30cm tart case

200g plain flour
50g rice flour
60g icing sugar
a pinch of salt
125g cold butter, cubed
2 medium egg yolks
1 tsp cold water

Tip the flours, icing sugar and salt into a food processor and pulse to separate and aerate the grains. Add the cold butter cubes and pulse again until the mix looks like fine breadcrumbs. Pour in the egg yolks along with the cold water and pulse again. The mixture will start to stick to the sides of the bowl and come together.

Take the crumbly mixture out and use your hands to bring it together on a clean work surface, working very quickly so as not to overwork it. Form the dough into a ball, wrap tightly in cling film, flatten it slightly and leave to chill in the fridge for at least one hour, preferably two hours.

Lightly dust the worktop with flour and roll the pastry evenly into a circle, turning it clockwise whilst rolling. Once the thickness is somewhere between a pound coin and a fifty pence piece, drape the pastry over the rolling pin and lower it over the tart tin. Gently unfold the pastry from the rolling pin. Press the pastry into the corners of the tin with your fingers and lightly stick a fork into the base a few times. Trim the edges by rolling the rolling pin over the top of the tart case where the pastry generously topples over the edge. Wrap any leftover bits in cling film and keep to plug any holes or cracks that may appear after blind baking. Chill the tart case and the leftovers in the fridge for thirty minutes.

Preheat the oven to 180°C/gas 6.

Line the chilled tart case with greaseproof paper and fill with baking beans. Blind bake for twenty minutes then remove the paper and beans and reduce the temperature to 160°C/gas 3 and bake for a further ten minutes until very pale golden. Remove from the oven and cool in the tin on a wire rack, ready for filling (see pages 231, 253, 274 and 282 for ideas).

Squillionaires' shortbread

So what makes this even better than millionaires' shortbread? Patting the nuts into the toffee takes away the overly sweet flavour while adding a knobbly, nutty, more substantial centre.

Makes fifteen squares

For the biscuit:
150g plain flour
100g semolina
75g icing sugar
a pinch of salt
200g butter,
   at room temperature

For the caramel:
175g butter
175g golden caster sugar
3 tbsp runny honey
1 x 397g tin of condensed milk

For the topping:
100g whole hazelnuts
200g dark chocolate
2 tsp coffee essence

Heat the oven to 170°C/gas 5 and lightly grease and line a 30cm x 20cm oblong tin.

In a large bowl mix the flour, semolina, icing sugar and salt. Rub in the butter with your fingertips until the mixture has the consistency of breadcrumbs. Tip onto a clean work surface and bring the dough together, gently kneading into a firm, slightly tacky ball. Press into the base of the tin and prick with a fork. Bake for twenty to thirty minutes until firm and lightly tanned. Set aside to cool.

Toast the hazelnuts on a baking tray for four minutes until the skins begin to crack and pop off. Pour them into a clean but damp tea towel, bringing the edges up to the centre to make a parcel. Roll the bundle over the work surface to loosen the blackened skins. Discard the skins, and roughly chop the hazelnuts, or bash using a mortar and pestle, then set aside.

In a heavy-bottomed pot, melt the butter, sugar, honey and condensed milk over a low heat, stirring until the butter has melted and sugar granules have dissolved. Turn up the heat to medium and allow the mixture to bubble away gently for five to eight minutes, stirring all the time to stop it catching, until it turns thick and fudgy. Be very careful of the lava-like bubbles as the mixture will be extremely hot.

Spread the hot caramel over the shortbread in an even layer. Scatter over the hazelnuts, using the back of a wooden spoon to press them in firmly. Leave to cool for about fifteen minutes. In the meantime, break the chocolate into small pieces and melt in a heatproof bowl over a pan of simmering water. Stir through the coffee essence and remove from the heat. Pour the chocolate over the caramel and leave to harden (roughly fifteen to thirty minutes).

When the chocolate has set, carefully take the edges of the greaseproof paper and prise the shortbread out of the tin onto a chopping board. Cut into smallish pieces since, like all squillionaires, it is very, very rich.

Jam roly-poly

I've always had a sweet tooth and tend to look at the dessert menu first when dining out. Roly-poly pudding was the only bit of school dinners I liked, although this version is obviously an improvement on the school recipe. Homemade jam is key, as is keeping the custard (page 227) that accompanies it skin-free. This recipe makes a couple of jars of really good thick jam. I always think it's worth making a decent quantity, so that you have plenty left over to enjoy on toast.

Serves six

For the raspberry jam:
400g jam sugar
juice of 1 unwaxed lemon
500g raspberries

For the roly-poly dough:
250g plain flour
2 tsp baking powder
a pinch of salt
1 tbsp light brown sugar
125g suet pieces
about 150ml milk

Pop a plate in the freezer and sterilise a couple of jars – just wash them, then place in the oven for ten minutes at 80°C/gas ¼ to dry.

Pour the sugar into a large non-reactive pan (not copper or aluminium) and squeeze in the lemon juice through a sieve to avoid any pips falling in. Keeping the heat very low, stir the sugary mixture to help it dissolve. After two minutes, tumble in half the raspberries and stir them through allowing everything to melt down and combine. Now turn the heat up and let the mixture bubble away for five minutes, stirring every so often to prevent it catching on the bottom of the pot.

Pour in the other half of the raspberries and boil the jam rapidly for a further five minutes, using a ladle to skim off any scum that may appear on the surface. Take the pan off the heat, take the plate out of the freezer and drop a little spoonful of the jam onto the cold plate. This is to test the texture: push your finger through the red sticky mixture; if you like it quite runny then bottle it now; if not, put the plate back in the freezer and the pan back on the heat. Boil the jam for another two minutes before testing again, by which time the jam should wrinkle when you push it with your finger.

Pour the jam into the jars, seal and set aside, ready to smear over the roly-poly.

Heat the oven to 200°C/gas 7.

Place the flour and baking powder in a large bowl. Combine with the salt, sugar and suet pieces and just enough milk to create a soft, but not sticky, dough. Don't worry if there's milk left over – you may not need all of it. Turn the dough out onto a floured surface and knead gently for about ten minutes until it becomes a tacky and springy ball.

Cut a large rectangular piece of greaseproof paper (at least 32cm x 24cm) and lightly rub with a little butter. Roll the dough into a rectangle about 28cm x 20cm and lift onto the buttered greaseproof paper. Dollop four tablespoons of the jam into the centre and spread it outwards, leaving a 2-3cm jam-free border.

Gently roll the dough up from the long side – fold the jam-free border tightly over where it meets the jam, then roll the rest of the dough up gently, making sure it finishes seam side down on the paper. Now take the edges of the greaseproof paper and carefully wrap the roly-poly loosely – remember it will expand when cooked. Twist the ends of the paper like a Christmas cracker and tie tightly at the ends with kitchen string to secure. Just to protect it further, wrap it loosely in a large piece of aluminium foil (again about 32cm x 24cm), twisting the ends like a cracker once more.

Place the rolled dough parcel onto a roasting rack set over a roasting tin. Trickle boiling water into the tin until about half full. Bake in the oven for thirty-five to forty minutes.

Carefully lift out the roasting tin and roly-poly parcel from the oven. Snip through the foil, string and greaseproof paper with scissors, folding back all the layers to reveal a risen, gilded roly-poly.

Please don't be disappointed if the jam has escaped through the dough; it will taste just as good and any imperfections can be covered up by a tablespoon of Demerara sugar sprinkled over the top. Place generous slices of the roly-poly into bowls and serve while piping hot with lots of custard (see page 227).

Three

I can still remember taking a bite of my father's ham sandwich as a child and feeling a hot, burning sensation hitting the roof of my mouth and nose. What was this sludgy yellow paste that had so overwhelmed my childish senses? It took me a while to find the courage to try mustard again, and that was not until much later in life.

The truth is I only began to appreciate mustard when I started working in a kitchen. The mustard arrived in vats that were nearly as big as me, and I was amazed at the different uses to which it was put. I had only really eaten mustard as a condiment before. Whilst working in the kitchen I realised that it's the backbone that not only stabilises but adds depth, warmth and roundness to basic sauces like mayonnaise, hollandaise, salsa verde, béarnaise, béchamel and many more.

It is a truly versatile ingredient, which is why it's so easy to add to a wide range of dishes and sauces. English, Dijon or wholegrain mustards are the perfect accompaniment to barbecued meats, hot dogs and ham sandwiches, are great added to a vinaigrette and absolutely essential when tucking into a steak or roast. The pungent richness cuts through fat and brings out the flavour of fleshy meats.

On an early trip to Venice I fell in love with 'tramezzini': the stuffed crustless sandwiches the Venetians love as little snacks or 'cicchetti'. They have a particular way of making a mustard sauce (a kind of 'Dijonnaise' made with a light mustard and mayonnaise) that they call 'salsa piccante'. It's very moreish with finely chopped ham.

Being a traditionalist I know that I should say I like English mustard, but although a good slather of it is sometimes called for, I much prefer Dijon's milder tones. I love wholegrain's more delicate taste too, and the way the seeds burst and pop between my teeth.

At home you can of course make a wide variety of mustards from their seeds. While there are over forty different varieties of mustard plant, the most commonly used seeds are black, brown or yellow in descending order of sharpness. These can be ground to a powder and mixed with a combination of cold water, wine or vinegar to make the familiar amber paste.

Mustard was the original British condiment long before curry, chilli or cumin arrived from across the seas. It was our way of adding heat to food before other spices were readily available. English mustard has become a tradition that means so much to so many of us, and the shelves of my cupboard are always brightened up by the iconic little yellow tin. The dry powder doesn't have much of a kick on its own, as the heat only comes into the taste once the water or wine has been added and a chemical reaction occurs.

Any good dish should have a beginning, middle and end note. Mustard comes in very handy as it holds that middle note perfectly. As long as it's used sparingly!

Simplicity is the key to great food. There's no doubt that many of us would place a hearty plate of sausages and mash at the top of our all-time favourite meals. I know I would. I don't know where a dish like this would be without a good smear of hot mustard.

Polpettine

I use a light touch to make these small Italian meatballs as otherwise they become too dense. I don't use eggs and instead soak the bread in milk and add mustard, using this to combine the mixture. The sauce is slow-cooked and improves with time. It is worth making a big batch of these, since polpettine go really well through pasta and in sandwiches, and you can store any extras in the freezer for a month or so.

Makes four small plates

For the sauce:
extra virgin olive oil
1 onion
a large pinch of salt
2 garlic cloves
a pinch of dried chilli
3 sprigs of thyme
3 sprigs of oregano
2 x 400g tin of plum tomatoes
zest of 1 unwaxed lemon

For the polpettine:
1 large onion
2 garlic cloves
a pinch of salt
2 sprigs of rosemary
3 sprigs of thyme
extra virgin olive oil
2 slices of bread (stale or fresh)
100ml milk
5g Parmesan, plus extra
1 tsp Dijon mustard
250g beef mince
120g pork mince
½ tsp dried chilli
fresh nutmeg, grated (to taste)

Heat a glug of olive oil in a heavy-bottomed pan on a low heat. Halve, peel and slice the onion. Add with the salt to the hot pan then reduce the heat and cook for ten minutes or so until soft. While the onions are cooking, peel and finely slice the garlic.

Stir through the garlic, chilli and herbs and cook for a minute, then add the tomatoes and their juices from the tins. Swill each of the emptied tins with a little water to get the last remnants of tomato and add this to the pan too. Increase the heat to high and simmer for a few minutes, avoiding the temptation to keep stirring. Then turn the heat down low and leave to reduce to a thick chunky texture. The longer you cook it, the better the sauce will be. I tend to leave it to simmer quietly for about thirty minutes to an hour while I make the meatballs.

While the sauce is reducing, make the polpettine. Peel the onion and garlic, dicing the onion as finely as you can. Using a mortar and pestle, grind the garlic with the salt to a smooth paste. Pick and finely chop the rosemary and thyme leaves.

Preheat the oven to 160°C/gas 4 and lightly grease a baking tray.

Put a pan on the heat with a little olive oil and sweat down the onion, garlic, rosemary and thyme. Once they're completely soft, spread them over a plate and put it in the fridge to cool.

Soak the bread in the milk in a shallow bowl for five to ten minutes until the milk has been absorbed. Grate the Parmesan on a fine setting. Once softened, break the bread into small chunks with your hands and discard any leftover milk.

Put the cooled onions and garlic, soaked bread, Parmesan, mustard, beef and pork mince, chilli and nutmeg in a large bowl and mix together with your hands. Be careful not to overwork the mixture. I like meatballs to be light and juicy, and overworking results in a very dense and heavy meatball. Grease your hands with a few drops of olive oil and then shape the mixture into balls about the size of giant marbles.

Place the polpettine on the greased baking tray and bake in the oven for ten minutes. They will still be soft when they come out — the baking is just to colour them and set their shape, not to cook them through which happens in the sauce.

Grate the lemon zest into the now-reduced sauce and add a splash of olive oil. Then add the polpettine to the sauce to simmer for a few minutes to cook through.

Serve on small plates and eat topped with finely grated Parmesan and a dash of olive oil.

Beef fillet, anchovy & mustard

This is actually a beef carpaccio, which was allegedly first made in Harry's Bar in Venice. The anchovy and mustard add a real touch of Venetian 'piccante'. I like to use Ortiz anchovies for this.

Makes four small plates

250g beef fillet
*1 large handful of lamb's
  lettuce*

For the dressing:
½ garlic clove
a pinch of salt
5 anchovy fillets
1 tbsp Dijon mustard
1 tbsp red wine vinegar
100ml extra virgin olive oil

Clean any tendon from the outside of the fillet, then wrap it in cling film and then a tea towel and chill the meat in the freezer for ten minutes to make it easier to slice.

Slice the chilled beef as thinly as you possibly can. Spread the slices on greaseproof paper, cover with another sheet of greaseproof and use a rolling pin or the flat of a heavy knife to batter them until they're just a couple of millimetres thick. Alternatively you can roll them with a heavy rolling pin to achieve the same effect.

Peel the garlic and grind it to a paste with the salt using a pestle and mortar. Add the anchovies and grind the mixture a little more, leaving it slightly chunky.

In a bowl, stir together the mustard and vinegar and season with salt and pepper. Slowly dribble in the olive oil, whisking until the dressing has the consistency of single cream. Stir through the garlic and anchovy paste, then use to dress the leaves lightly in a separate bowl.

Drape the beef on the plates and scatter over the leaves, with a little more of the dressing dribbled over to serve.

Buttered mustard lobster

Mustard could overpower delicate seafood, but this milder mustard powder encloses the lobster meat with a crust that retains the moisture of the flesh. I love scooping the pink meat out of the coral-coloured shell. I always buy lobsters live to ensure that they are as fresh as possible. Placing them in the freezer for twenty to thirty minutes before cooking should make them dormant, and I also cover them with a damp tea towel to protect their eyes, which are very sensitive.

Makes four small ramekins

2 lobsters
1 small bunch of
  flat-leaf parsley
2 slices of stale bread
2 heaped tsp English
  mustard powder
2 tbsp crème fraiche
½ tbsp butter
1 unwaxed lemon, in wedges

Carefully place the lobsters in the freezer with a damp tea towel over their eyes. While the lobsters are chilling, fill a large pan with cold water, add a good pinch of salt and place it on a high heat.

Once the water is boiling rapidly, take the lobsters out of the freezer and lower them head first into the hot water, ensuring that they are fully submerged. Boil for three minutes then turn the heat down and simmer for another three minutes. Remove the lobsters from the water and set aside until cool enough to handle.

While the lobsters are cooling, pick and chop the parsley leaves. Tear the bread roughly and blitz to fine crumbs in a processor.

Lay the lobsters on their backs and, with very sharp knife, cleave each in half lengthways. Remove the black sac from the head and throw it away. Dislodge the body meat and remove and discard the black vein running the length of the tail. Crack the claws and scoop out the meat.

Chop the lobster meat roughly, put in a bowl and stir together with the parsley, breadcrumbs, mustard powder and crème fraiche. Season lightly.

Turn the grill on to a high heat. Spoon the mixture into heatproof ramekins or bowls and top each with a little knob of butter. Place under the hot grill for about five to ten minutes until the mixture bubbles up and becomes crisp on top. Serve with a lemon wedge on the side to squeeze over.

Bacon & egg baked asparagus with lovage

This is especially gooey. It's baked in crème fraiche and mustard, which adds a necessary sourness to this otherwise rich dish. Cutting into the runny yolk is so satisfying. A real crowd-pleaser for Sunday brunch.

For two to share, or one very hungry person

2 slices of slightly stale bread
40g Gruyère
2 sprigs of thyme
10 white asparagus spears
1 capful of white vinegar
3 heaped tbsp crème fraiche
2 tsp wholegrain mustard
extra virgin olive oil
4 rashers of bacon
1 large egg
black pepper, to taste
2 stems of lovage

Preheat the oven to 200°C/gas 7.

Start by tearing the bread roughly into small pieces into a bowl. Grate in the Gruyère, pick the thyme leaves and scatter over and then set aside. Snap the ends off the asparagus.

Put a pan of water on to boil and add the vinegar. Melt the crème fraiche and mustard together in a small pan over a low heat.

Put a frying pan with a metal handle (or one that can go in the oven) on the heat and add a little olive oil. While the oil is heating up, wrap each rasher of bacon around a bunch of two or three asparagus spears, then fry the bacon bundles in the hot pan. After a couple of minutes when the bacon starts to crisp up, pour over the crème fraiche mixture and scatter on the bread pieces and thyme. Place the pan in the oven to bake for ten minutes until the asparagus is tender and the bread pieces are golden.

Now poach the egg while the gratin bakes. Crack the egg into a little cup. Turn the boiling water down to a simmer. Swirl the water and gently tip the egg into the centre of the swirl. Cook for a couple of minutes until the white has set then remove with a slotted spoon.

Place the egg on top of the gratin and crack over a little black pepper. Pick and roughly tear the lovage leaves, then scatter over to garnish. Eat this dish straight from the pan.

Ox tongue with Anya potatoes & green sauce

The first time I prepared this, it was daunting. Ox tongue is huge and a little bit gross. It takes a little getting used to, but don't be squeamish. It's a cheap cut with a firm meaty texture, and there's a reason why it's been eaten for thousands of years. You will need to start cooking this recipe at least four days in advance of serving, to allow sufficient time for brining the tongue.

Makes six small plates

1 whole ox tongue
  (roughly 1kg)

To brine the tongue:
450g golden caster sugar
700g salt
10 black peppercorns
8 juniper berries
4 garlic cloves, peeled
6 bay leaves
about 5l water

To cook the tongue:
2 onions
½ head of celery
1 leek
2 carrots
2 bay leaves
parsley stalks (see green sauce)
3 garlic cloves
5 black peppercorns

For the potatoes:
800g Anya potatoes
100g butter
2 sprigs of fresh mint
1 bunch of mustard leaves

Put the tongue into a very large non-reactive pan (not aluminium or copper) with all the brining ingredients and cover with cold water (about 5 litres), making sure the tongue is fully submerged. Cook over a low heat until the sugar and salt have dissolved, then bring the brine to the boil. Simmer for five minutes, then remove from the heat and allow it to cool.

Soak the tongue in the cold brine in the covered pan for three to five days. Then remove the tongue from the brine and soak in fresh water for at least twelve hours, changing the water at least twice during that time.

When you come to cook the tongue, rinse it and place in a large pan. Peel and halve the onions, separate the celery into sticks, chop the leek into chunky disks and chop the carrot into large chunks. Place these in the large pan with the bay leaves, parsley stalks, garlic and peppercorns and enough water to cover everything. Bring to the boil then reduce the heat to a very gentle simmer and cook for three and a half hours.

The cooked tongue will need to be peeled, so a good test as to whether it is cooked sufficiently is to see whether the skin comes away easily. You will need to peel it while it is still warm otherwise it will be almost impossible. A pair of rubber gloves will probably help here to give you some heat protection! The skin should peel off like a sock, and you will need to trim away the gristle at the tongue root. Leave the peeled tongue to cool completely and then slice as thinly as you can.

Place the potatoes in a pan with enough cold water to cover them, along with the butter, mint and a generous pinch of salt. Boil the potatoes gently until tender.

For the green sauce:
1 garlic clove
a pinch of sea salt
2 tsp capers
3 anchovy fillets
1 small bunch of flat-leaf
 parsley (leaves only)
6 sprigs of fresh mint
1 tbsp Dijon mustard
1 tbsp white wine vinegar
3 tbsp extra virgin olive oil

While the potatoes are boiling, make the green sauce. Use a mortar and pestle to grind up the peeled garlic with the salt. Add the capers and anchovies and grind the mixture to a coarse paste. Add the parsley and mint leaves and grind again, leaving them quite coarse. Stir through the mustard, vinegar and olive oil.

Check the potatoes after fifteen to twenty minutes – once a knife falls through them easily, they're ready – then drain and halve any of the bigger potatoes. Place in a large serving bowl. Wash the mustard leaves in cold water and scatter them through the potatoes.

Loosely fold the slices of ox tongue through the warm potatoes and mustard leaves and generously spoon over the green sauce before serving.

Smoked sausage, maple chicory & lentils

This dish makes me think of woolly jumpers, sheepskin rugs, and roaring fires. It's my Italian version of bangers and mash – cosy, familiar and hearty. I like to use smoked Toulouse sausages from the Ginger Pig.

Makes four small plates

6 smoked Toulouse sausages

For the lentils:
250g Puy lentils
1 onion
1 garlic clove
1 bay leaf
600ml chicken or vegetable stock (or water)
1 tbsp extra virgin olive oil

For the chicory:
a pinch of salt
1 tbsp caster sugar
1 unwaxed lemon
4 small heads of chicory
50g butter
50ml maple syrup
4 sprigs of thyme

For the mustard dressing:
2 tsp Dijon mustard
1 tsp runny honey
1 tsp lemon juice, reserved
1 tbsp extra virgin olive oil
1 tsp red wine vinegar, to finish

Put the lentils in a pan, cover with cold water and boil on a high heat for ten minutes. Drain the lentils and rinse under cold running water until it runs clean, then tip them into a fresh pan.

Peel and halve the onion, peel and bash the garlic and add them to the lentils with the bay leaf. Cover with the stock and cook for twenty minutes until the lentils are soft and tender and most of the stock has been absorbed. Stir through a tablespoon of extra virgin olive oil and season to taste. Pop a lid on and set aside.

Preheat the oven to 200°C/gas 7.

For the chicory, fill a pan with cold water, add the salt and sugar and place over a high heat. Halve the lemon and squeeze the juice into the water, reserving one teaspoon for the dressing, then throw the lemon halves in too. Add the whole chicory and simmer for five minutes, then drain and rinse under cold running water. Run a knife down the centre of each chicory head to halve them. Cut out the heavy root from the bottom, being very careful to make sure that the leaves still hold together, then gently squeeze out any excess water. Season the chicory halves.

Heat the butter in an ovenproof pan and when it foams, place the chicory cut-side down in it. Cook in the bubbling butter over a medium heat for five minutes until the underside begins to colour. Pour over the maple syrup, scatter over the thyme sprigs and place in the oven for seven minutes until auburn-coloured and tender. Baste the chicory with the maple butter then cover with foil and leave in a warm place until you are ready to serve.

Place a large pan of water on to boil (big enough to fit the sausages). Boil the sausages for eight minutes in their skins then remove from the water and set aside to cool.

While the sausages are cooling, mix the mustard, honey and the reserved teaspoon of lemon juice in a small bowl, season to taste and then gradually whisk in the olive oil.

Run a knife down each sausage, then pull back and discard the skin. Crumble the meat into small morsel-sized chunks.

Drain the lentils if they need it. Pour over the dressing, the maple syrup-butter mixture from the chicory pan and the vinegar and stir well to combine. Fold through the warm chicory halves and finally crumble over the sausage before serving.

Venison, celeriac & cobnuts

I first tasted venison in a professional kitchen. It's not something my mother would ever have dreamt of cooking at home. It reminds me of a really well-aged beef, only with a slightly gamey flavour. Most of all it is incredibly lean and tender. The cobnut is a British delicacy and an ingredient to celebrate, lovely even eaten on its own with a little salt. If you can't lay your hands on cobnuts, use their siblings, hazelnuts, instead.

Makes four small plates

360g venison loin fillet
50g cobnuts
½ celeriac
juice of ½ unwaxed lemon
salt
a pinch of black pepper
extra virgin olive oil
2 tbsp crème fraiche
3–4 tsp wholegrain mustard

Preheat the oven to 180°C/gas 6. Take the meat out of the fridge to bring it to room temperature. Shell the cobnuts using a nutcracker.

Peel the celeriac with a small knife, carefully cut it into manageable pieces and slice thinly on a mandolin or with a sharp knife. Place the celeriac in a large bowl, squeeze the lemon juice over it and sprinkle with a pinch of salt.

Heat a splash of olive oil in a heavy-bottomed pan. Rub the venison with a pinch of salt and pepper. Once the pan is really hot, brown the meat on all sides, including the ends – you don't want to cook it through, as it should be rare in the centre, so just make sure that there is a good dark colour all over the outside. Place the pan in the oven for five minutes, then cover in foil and set aside to rest.

While the venison is resting, put the cobnuts on a dry baking or roasting tray and toast them in the oven for three to four minutes. Set them aside to cool.

Mix the crème fraiche and mustard through the celeriac.

Slice the venison as thinly as you can and combine it loosely together with the celeriac, cobnuts and another smattering of olive oil before serving.

Sausages & polenta

This is simple, honest cooking at its best. The wet polenta combines well with the fattiness of the sausages and the mustard binds the dish and adds depth. I like my polenta extra-runny.

Makes four large bowls

For the polenta:
1 onion
1.25l milk
2 bay leaves
4 black peppercorns
80g butter
100g quick cook polenta
50g Pecorino cheese
1 tbsp mascarpone

For the sausages:
olive oil
8 Toulouse sausages
2 onions
a pinch of salt
6 slices of pancetta
2 tsp Dijon mustard
3 sprigs of thyme
250ml white wine

Preheat the oven to 180°C/gas 6.

Begin by peeling and halving the onion for the polenta. Pour the milk into a saucepan containing the halved onion, bay leaves and peppercorns and simmer gently for fifteen minutes. Remove from the heat and leave to infuse.

Heat a little olive oil over a medium heat in a heavy-bottomed pan (one that that has a lid). Add the sausages, turning them occasionally until they have a rich dark colour on all sides. While they're browning, peel, halve and slice the onions into half-moon slivers and add to the pan with a pinch of salt. Cook the onion slowly for ten minutes or until soft, with the lid of the pan on to help the onions sweat.

Turn the heat up a little, remove the lid and add the pancetta. Stir through the mustard, scatter over the thyme, pour over the white wine and simmer everything for five minutes. Stick the lid back on the pan and place it in the oven for twenty minutes.

While the sausages are cooking in the oven, prepare the polenta. Strain the milk, discarding the bay leaves, peppercorns and onion, and then return it to the saucepan. Place the saucepan on a high heat and add the butter. When the butter has melted, very slowly whisk in the polenta and turn the heat right down. Cook the polenta for fifteen to twenty minutes until the granules have dissolved, stirring non-stop. Finely grate in the Pecorino and stir through the mascarpone.

Spoon the polenta into bowls, place a couple of sausages and a ladleful of the juice on each and serve straight away.

Salt beef with braised leeks in mustard

Although age-old, salting is still one of the tastiest ways to cook, flavour and tenderise a cheap cut of meat. It is a lengthy process (you will need to allow three days' brining before you can cook the beef) but an easy one, and yields wonderful results. You don't hear enough about grey salt. It hasn't been through any bleaching processes, is a reasonable price and has a wonderful flavour. I haven't tried to reinvent the wheel here – salt beef demands mustard, but rather than just a dollop on the side of your plate, it works beautifully braised slowly into the leeks to embolden the sauce.

Makes six to eight large plates

2kg beef brisket

To brine the beef:
180g soft light brown sugar
250g grey salt
6 black peppercorns
2 juniper berries
3 garlic cloves
4 bay leaves
2l water

To cook the beef:
1 onion
1 large carrot
2 sticks of celery
1 leek
2 bay leaves

For the leeks:
10 leeks
1 tbsp Dijon mustard
2 tbsp wholegrain mustard
480ml chicken stock
50g butter
2 bay leaves
150ml double cream

Put all the ingredients for the brine in a large saucepan over a low heat, stirring every so often to help the sugar and salt to dissolve. Gradually bring to the boil and let it bubble away for five minutes, then take the pan off the heat and leave the mixture to cool completely.

Sterilise a deep tray or bucket made of a non-reactive material (not aluminium or copper) by scrubbing it with baking soda and then rinsing with boiling water. Trim any excess fat off the brisket. Pierce the meat all over with the tip of a knife and place in the tray or bucket. Cover the meat with the cold brine, making sure it's totally submerged, weighing the brisket down with a heavy plate if necessary. Cover the container and squeeze it into the fridge or leave in a cold room for three days.

Pull the meat out of the brine and give it a good rinse under cold running water. Place the brisket in a large pan and cover with cold water. Peel and halve the onion and roughly chop the carrot, celery and leek. Place them in the pan with the bay leaves. Bring the water to a gentle simmer and allow to bubble away slowly uncovered for two to three hours, until the meat flakes apart into large chunks.

Once the beef has been simmering for about an hour and a half, wash and trim the leeks, removing the roots, leafy green tops and outer skin. Cut them into 5cm-wide hoops and sit them upright tightly packed in a shallow casserole pot.

Mix the mustards and chicken stock and pour over the leeks. Dollop over the butter, add the bay leaves and season. Place the pan on a medium heat and bring to the boil, then simmer for twenty minutes to reduce the liquid by two thirds.

Preheat the oven to 170°C/gas 5.

Lower the heat under the leeks to a gentle simmer (so that the cream won't split when added). Once the leeks are simmering rather than boiling, pour over the cream. Place the leeks in the oven and bake for twenty-five minutes.

To serve, spoon generous helpings of the leeks and the creamy mustard sauce over thick slices of the salt beef.

Whole roasted veal shin with broad beans

Slow cooking is very little work and the meat ends up falling off the bone (not to mention getting stuck in your teeth). Milk and mustard is an unusual way to cook broad beans and you have to be careful that it doesn't curdle, but this method plumps and softens the tough skins that you normally peel away, so they can be eaten too.

Makes four large plates

For the veal:
1.5kg veal shin, on the bone
extra virgin olive oil
1 onion
1 bulb of fennel
1 head of celery
4 sprigs of thyme
2 bay leaves
a pinch of salt
200ml white wine
250ml chicken stock

For the broad beans:
1 tbsp extra virgin olive oil
3 garlic cloves
500g broad beans
8 sage leaves
1 tbsp wholegrain mustard
300ml milk
zest of 2 unwaxed lemons

Take the shin out of the fridge and leave to come to room temperature. Preheat the oven to 180°C/gas 6.

Heat a tablespoon of olive oil in a heavy-bottomed pan. Once it is hot, place the veal in for a couple of minutes, cooking each side until caramelised and a rich brown. Remove the shin and transfer it to a large casserole pan with a well-fitting lid.

While the meat is browning, peel, halve and dice the onion. Discard the outer layers and trim away the tips and hard bases of the fennel bulb and celery head, then halve them.

Pour another glug of olive oil into the heavy-bottomed pan that you browned the veal in, place over a low heat and add the onion, fennel, celery, thyme, bay leaves and a pinch of salt. Sweat down for eight minutes until the vegetables soften and begin to caramelise.

Pour over the wine and stock and let the mixture bubble away for a minute or two, then carefully pour everything into the casserole pan around the veal shin. Cover and place in the oven for two and a half hours, until the meat is falling off the bone.

While the veal is slow cooking, heat up the olive oil for the broad beans in a thick-bottomed pan over a medium heat. Use the flat of a knife to crush the garlic cloves and discard the skins. Add the garlic and broad beans to the oil and cook slowly for a few minutes until the garlic begins to colour.

Add the sage, stir through the mustard and pour over the milk. Cover the pan and lower the heat to a very gentle simmer so as not to curdle the milk. Simmer for eight minutes until the beans are tender and have absorbed most of the liquid. Grate over the lemon zest and season to taste. To serve, fork large pieces of the veal onto warmed plates and spoon over the juicy beans.

Four

I start my working day in a cloud of vinegar, when one part vinegar is added to one part water and poured over the hot grill behind me to clear off any residual grease before the day's cooking begins. The vapour fills the kitchen with that unmistakable aroma, and always makes my eyes smart.

Distilled vinegar has been used for centuries for cleaning and disinfecting. To be honest, these are probably the best uses for the cheap chemically-produced variety. I use it for everything from clearing smeared windows to removing stains from the insides of my teacups and it's become a regular routine to get rid of lime deposits in my kettle. I have even been known to drink a capful to cure myself of hiccups.

Alone, vinegar can be too acidic, but it has a wide range of flavours; some thin and eye-wateringly sharp, others rich, mellow, and sometimes sweet. It is one of the oldest fermented food products known to man and is only predated by wine. There are many different kinds of vinegar but my favourite is Moscatel vinegar from Tarragona in Spain. It has nothing to do with the similarly named Muscatel, a cheap white wine made from the muscat grape. A drop or two of Moscatel will make all the difference to a dish, adding a fruity but gentle sharpness.

Other than that, I like to use well-aged balsamic vinegar. Balsamic traditionally has a rich syrupy consistency and has been made in Modena, Italy, for centuries using the time-tested methods. This involves the boiling and aging of Trebbiano grapes in a succession of progressively smaller barrels over many years. It is highly prized for its distinctive bold taste. Tearing bread and submerging it in a puddle of mellow balsamic is one of the loveliest ways to start any meal.

Often good quality red, and sometimes white, wine vinegars are called for in dressings but I like to use these more broadly. A spoonful goes very far and is especially good for tenderising and marinating thinly-carved fish.

A fine sherry vinegar is a potent base for a quick marinade for meats and can be used as a substitute for the more expensive balsamic variety.

Italian cooking, and Venetian cooking in particular, uses a lot of vinegar. It's normally combined with sugar and reduced in a hot pan to produce a sweet and sour sauce known as 'agrodolce'. 'Agro' means sour and 'dolce' sweet.

The Venetians have developed 'agrodolce' over the years by adding various other ingredients such as sweet onions and sultanas and using it to marinate fish and meats. Their 'sarde in saor' for instance is a traditional method of preserving sardines.

Like the Italians, I use vinegar a lot. I love to pickle things and I've experimented with almost every fruit and vegetable known to man. For me there is just nothing more satisfying than seeing my jars of chutney and pickles full of summer produce stretching across the shelves of my cupboard like little soldiers, with their contents glinting through the pickling juice, amber and golden in the autumn light. A good pickle should have a light, sweet mellow sharpness and should not be lip-smarting or too acidic.

Who can forget the tangy sharpness that malt vinegar brings to a simple bag of fish and chips? But remember, there is more to it than acidity; vinegar comes in many forms but it always adds a distinct depth of flavour to any dish. So it's time to celebrate vinegar, whether you use it to marinate a raw fish, dress crisp salad leaves, pickle fruits or even clean cutlery.

Burrata, pickled beetroot & rhubarb

Mozzarella can be tasteless and rubbery, and not even buffalo mozzarella compares to burrata, which is softer, moister and creamier and so can carry big flavours like pickles. Always serve burrata at room temperature rather than chilled. It is always best to buy large ones to split so you have more of the creamy centre, which is the best bit. Burrata is an exquisite ingredient to work with and I never take it off the menu; it pairs well with so many ingredients, from pink stripey Chioggia beetroot and celeriac in the winter to broad beans and peas in the summer and even rhubarb and beetroot in autumn. I simply love it.

Makes eight small plates

*For the pickled beetroot
and rhubarb:*
*1 large Chioggia or
ordinary beetroot*
2 sticks of champagne rhubarb
300ml white wine vinegar
125ml water
100g caster sugar, plus 50g
1 clove
1 bay leaf

2 x 250g burrata
fruity extra virgin olive oil

Peel the beetroot bulb, slice the whole beetroot very thinly with a mandolin and set aside in a bowl. Trim the rhubarb, discarding the white leafy top and dry end, and cut into 5cm sticks. Place the sticks in a separate container.

Put the vinegar, water, 100g of sugar, clove and bay leaf into a small pan over a low heat and stir to help dissolve the sugar. Once the sugar has dissolved, remove half of the liquor and cool it in a separate container. If you pour the liquor over the beetroot when it's hot, the coloured ring of the Chioggia leaches into the white flesh so you lose the stripy effect.

Now add the extra 50g of sugar to the remaining half of the liquor and simmer again until it has dissolved. Bring to the boil then pour it over the rhubarb sticks. Cover tightly with foil or cling film and set aside in a warm place for thirty minutes to an hour until the rhubarb sticks are tender but not falling apart.

Once the other half of the liquor has lowered to room temperature, pour it over the sliced beetroot and leave for twenty to thirty minutes.

Tear each burrata into quarters and divide between the plates, making sure everyone gets an even amount of gooey centre. Spoon over the rhubarb and beetroot with a little of the pink pickling liquor and a dribble of a fine fruity olive oil.

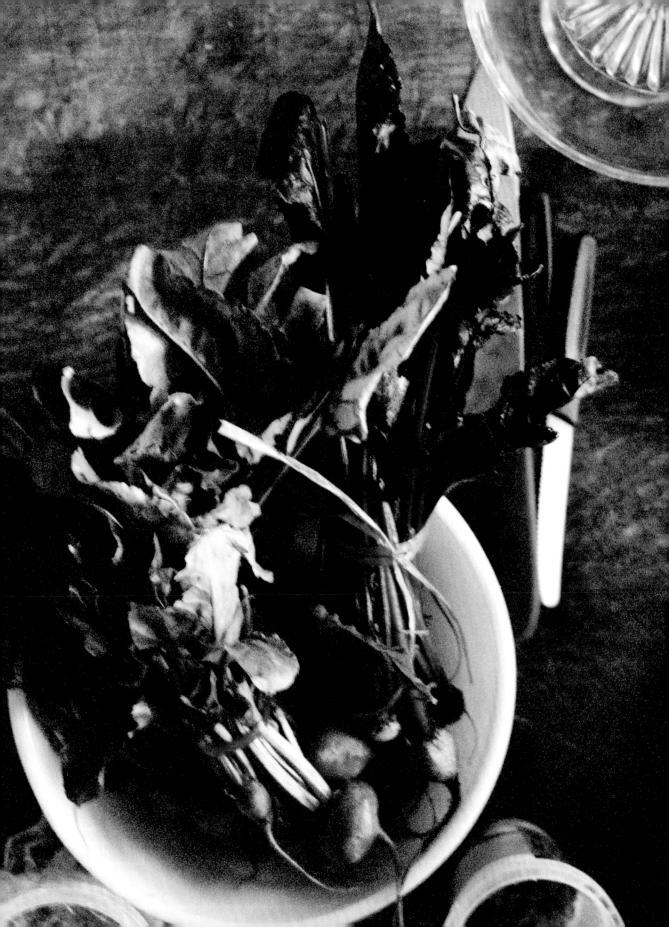

Prawns in saor

This is based on the Venetian classic marinated sardine dish 'sarde in saor', which typifies the region's fascination with sweet and sour flavours. Saor dishes improve with time: here the vinegar mellows and helps soften the skin of the prawns while the raisins puff up from drinking all the juices. I could graze on this for days. Make a large batch and store it away – it is best made a day or two in advance and will keep for about a week in the fridge.

Makes four small plates

5 medium onions
extra virgin olive oil
2 bay leaves
8 black peppercorns
a pinch of salt
100g pine nuts
about 350ml white
    wine vinegar
100g raisins
1l vegetable oil, for frying
a small piece of bread
450g fresh prawns
3 tbsp plain flour

Preheat the oven to 180°C/gas 6.

Peel, halve and finely slice the onions.

Place a glug of olive oil in a large heavy-bottomed pan (with a lid) over a very low heat. Drop in the sliced onions, bay leaves, peppercorns and salt, cover with the lid and allow everything to sweat for about thirty minutes until soft and colourless.

While the onions are sweating, toast the pine nuts in the oven on a dry baking tray for a few minutes until they are a light burnished gold. Remove from the oven and set aside to cool.

Once the onions are sticky-soft with no colour, pour over enough white wine vinegar to completely submerge them and stir through the raisins. Cook out the vinegar slowly, uncovered, until the onions have absorbed nearly all of the liquid. The mixture should look like a very thick French onion soup.

While the vinegar is cooking down, heat the vegetable oil in a heavy-bottomed saucepan over a medium heat for about twenty minutes or until it reaches 175°C. To test whether the oil is hot enough, put a little piece of bread in the pan to see whether it becomes crispy.

Peel the prawns while the oil is heating up – remove the heads but leave the tails attached. Tip the flour onto a plate, season with salt and pepper and toss through with your fingers to combine. Dust each prawn in the seasoned flour and shake off any excess.

Lower the prawns into the pan, being careful not to overcrowd them, and fry until they're golden brown. You may need to do this in several batches, depending on the size of your pan. Once cooked, fish the prawns out with a slotted spoon, drain them off and place them on the kitchen roll to remove any excess oil.

Give the onions a stir, remove from the heat and fold through the pine nuts. Spoon half the onions into a container (at least 3cm deep) then scatter the prawns on top. Cover with the remaining onions and pat down slightly. Let it all cool down then cover and leave in the fridge overnight to mellow.

Eat, preferably at room temperature, with crunchy bread.

Braised haricot beans & lardo

I'm not ashamed to admit that I like Heinz Baked Beans, but once you've tried my homemade variety you'll never look back. Lardo is a variety of extra-fatty ham from Tuscany. Here it adds a salty, meaty taste as well as a satiny texture that melts into the beans, while the vinegar provides a beautifully subtle aftertaste.

Makes four small plates

400g dried haricot beans
1 tsp bicarbonate of soda
extra virgin olive oil
1 onion
a pinch of salt
2 garlic cloves
½ tsp dried chilli
1 unwaxed lemon
1 x 400g tin of plum tomatoes
2 tbsp Moscatel vinegar
1.5l chicken stock
4 sprigs of thyme
2 sprigs of oregano
8 pieces of thinly sliced lardo
black pepper, to taste

Soak the haricot beans overnight in cold water with a teaspoon of bicarbonate of soda. In the morning, drain them in a colander and rinse thoroughly under cold running water.

Place a saucepan on the hob on a low heat and add two tablespoons of olive oil. Peel and roughly dice the onion and add it to the pan with a pinch of salt. Cook slowly for ten minutes.

While the onions are softening, peel and slice the garlic. When the onions are tender, add the garlic and chilli. Shave in two pieces of lemon peel, stir it all through to combine, and leave to cook for a few minutes to allow the flavours to infuse.

Add the beans, tomatoes and their juices (rinse and swill the tins with a tiny bit of water and add this too), vinegar, stock, thyme, oregano and a glug of olive oil. Cover the pan and place it on a medium heat. When the mixture comes to the boil, remove the lid and turn the heat down. Simmer gently for up to an hour, checking regularly after about thirty minutes. You want the beans to absorb most of the liquid so that they will be soft enough to enjoy.

Ladle into shallow bowls with the lardo slices laid over the top and serve with a crack of black pepper, a dribble of olive oil and crunchy bread for dipping.

Beetroot & goat's curd

I feel like the American abstract painter Jackson Pollock when I plate this – splodging the deep purple paste over the plate, then dolloping the goat's curd. A work of art.

Makes four small plates

*4 medium purple beetroot
(about 350g)*
salt
4 sprigs of thyme
extra virgin olive oil
3 banana shallots
2 garlic cloves
1 fresh bay leaf
100g butter
2 tbsp Moscatel vinegar
125g goat's curd

For the herby sauce:
8 sprigs of thyme
6 sprigs of oregano
salt
1 tsp red wine vinegar
3 tbsp extra virgin olive oil

Preheat the oven to 200°C/gas 7.

Cut off the beetroot leaves and scrub the bulbs under cold running water. Tear four squares of tin foil, each large enough to wrap a beetroot in. Place each bulb in the centre of a foil square with a pinch of salt, a sprig of thyme and a drop of olive oil and tightly wrap into a parcel. Place in a roasting tin with two to three centimetres of water and bake for forty-five minutes until tender.

While the beetroot is baking, peel, halve and dice the shallots and roughly crush the garlic – this doesn't have to be perfect as it'll be blitzed later. Heat two tablespoons of olive oil in a heavy-bottomed pan with, add the shallots with a pinch of salt and cook for ten minutes until soft but without colour. Stir through the garlic and bay and cook for a further five minutes. Dollop in the butter and set aside.

Pick the thyme and oregano leaves and place in a mortar with a few pinches of salt. Pound the leaves until completely crushed. Stir in the vinegar. Slowly add the olive oil, stirring until it becomes a coarse but runny paste. Season and set aside.

Now carefully unwrap each parcel. Put the bulbs into a large bowl and cover with cling film for ten minutes (to help the beetroot skin to come away more easily). Peel by taking each bulb and pushing your fingers down its sides to push away the blackened skin. Discard the skin but keep any purple liquor. Roughly chop the bulbs, stir through the buttery shallot mixture and pour in any purple cooking liquor.

Pour the beetroot-shallot mixture into a blender or food processor and whizz with the Moscatel vinegar, two tablespoons of olive oil, a splash of warm water and a pinch of salt until it all becomes a smooth glossy paste.

To serve, smear a thick layer of the purple paste over each plate, then blob over the goat's curd and a smidgen of the herby sauce. Eat with chunky pieces of sourdough.

Sea bream & caraway

Plates of raw seafood, simply dressed with lemon and olive oil, are a common sight in Venice. Ensure your fish is really fresh with red gills and clear eyes, and take time to slice it as thinly as possible. The vinegar softens and effectively cooks the fish, so don't spoon it over until you are ready to serve. The caraway seeds have a warm, peppery fragrance that complements the sea bream. This recipe also works well using the juice of half a lemon instead of the vinegar, if you fancy a change.

*Makes four small or
two large plates*

*1 tsp caraway seeds
1 tbsp extra virgin olive oil
2 tsp Moscatel vinegar
a pinch of salt
1 x 500g sea bream, filleted*

Toast the caraway seeds in a small dry pan over a medium-high heat for two or three minutes until they're fragrant. Transfer to a small plate to cool and set aside.

Mix the olive oil, vinegar and salt together in a small bowl.

Place the fish skin-side down onto a chopping board. Run your finger over the fillet to make sure there are no bones that will interrupt your knife motion. If you find any, pull them out with tweezers.

Using a flexible or filleting knife, slice into the flesh at the tail-end – not right through but leaving a couple of millimetres so that the skin stays intact. Turn the blade so that the sharpened edge is facing towards the head of the fish and, firmly placing your hand flat on top of the fish, run the knife along towards the head to separate the fillet from the skin. Throw the skin away.

Carve the fish in thin slices and drape them over the plates, allowing the slices to fall with a few folds to give some height. Spoon over the Moscatel dressing, sprinkle over the seeds and serve at once.

Slow-cooked bobby beans

The English bobby bean is fatter than your regular French or Kenyan bean and slightly sweeter. It's an almost forgotten variety, but I think it is far superior to its foreign rivals. I love eating them raw, but they are even better braised in wine. Don't be frightened of losing that vibrant green colour. You want them to slow cook so they wilt and soak up all the winey juices.

Makes six small plates

2 large onions
3 garlic cloves
6 ripe plum tomatoes
3 tbsp extra virgin olive oil, plus extra
2 bay leaves
a pinch of salt
300g yellow bobby beans
400g green bobby beans
550ml white wine
2 tbsp red wine vinegar
6 sprigs of flat-leaf parsley
100ml vegetable stock

Put a large pan of water on to the boil. Peel, halve and finely slice the onions into half-moon slivers. Crush the garlic cloves with the flat of a knife and discard the skins.

Cut a small cross on the bottom of the tomatoes with a serrated knife and lower them into the boiling water. Blanch for a minute or so, but be careful not to leave the tomatoes too long as you do not want them to cook. Remove the tomatoes from the boiling water and pop them in a bowl of iced water. The skins should begin to shrivel and fall off a little on their own but you will need to give them a little help, so tease off the rest of the skin with your fingers. Once skinless, you can halve and de-seed the tomatoes, discarding the wet centres.

Heat the olive oil in heavy-bottomed pan. Add the onions along with the bay leaves and a good pinch of salt. Cook slowly for about ten to fifteen minutes over a low heat to avoid the onions taking on any colour. While the onions are cooking, pick the stalks off the beans, leaving the curly ends intact.

Once the onions are sticky and soft, add the garlic and cook for three minutes, stirring occasionally. Add the yellow beans, half the tomatoes, the wine and the vinegar and stir to combine. Increase the heat to high and leave to bubble for twenty minutes. Then add the green beans, parsley, stock and the rest of the tomatoes and allow to bubble for a further ten minutes, driving off the acidic flavour and reducing the liquor. By this time, the ingredients should have collapsed and soaked up all the juices. The beans won't be a vibrant bright green, in fact this is the exception to the usual rule – you want them to turn a sludgy green! Season well with salt and freshly ground black pepper.

Eat ladled into bowls, finished simply with a final dash of olive oil, or as a side with grilled meat or fish.

Mussels, cannellini beans & wild garlic

Wild garlic covers the woodland near where I grew up. It pops up from late winter to spring and has a beautiful white flower. Like regular garlic, it has a pungent smell that scents your hands, but unlike regular garlic, it has a milder taste, and you eat the leaves rather than the bulb. My mum supplies Polpetto with bundles of the stuff.

Makes four small plates

500g mussels
1 garlic clove
1 red chilli
2 tbsp extra virgin olive oil, plus extra
75ml white wine
2 tsp Moscatel vinegar
½ x 400g tin of cannellini beans
1 handful of wild garlic

Scrub any barnacles or bits of seaweed off the mussels under cold running water. Taking a mussel in your palm, grasp its beard and yank it towards the hinge of the shell. The beard should come off easily and be discarded, along with any open shells. Place the mussels in a bowl with a centimetre of cold water and cover with a damp cloth. Store in the fridge until ready to use.

Heat a large wide pan (one with a lid) over a medium flame. As it heats up, peel and slice the garlic and de-seed and dice the chilli. Pour the olive oil, garlic and chilli into the pan and cook for one minute to infuse the oil a little.

Turn the heat up and add the mussels, wine and vinegar. Place the lid on the pan and cook for two minutes, shaking the pan from time to time as the mussels pop open.

Drain and rinse the cannellini beans. Add the beans to the mussels, stir through and let it all simmer and bubble away for a few minutes until the beans are hot through. Then fold through the wild garlic, popping the lid back on for a minute or so until the garlic leaves have wilted a little and the last of the mussels has popped open. Discard any mussels that haven't opened after this time.

Season, then eat from shallow bowls with a dribble of extra virgin olive oil and bread for dipping.

Pickled damsons

*Autumn brings a glut of damsons, which are marvellous for pickling.
A close sibling of the plum, damsons are extremely tart and need sugar.
Eat them with venison, beef or as a topping for vanilla ice cream with
a dribble of honey. Use under-ripe damsons for this, if possible, because
they hold their shape rather than turning to mush.*

Makes one large jar

500g damsons
175ml white wine vinegar
225g caster sugar
3 cloves
2 black peppercorns

Rinse the damsons under cold running water, remove any stalks or
leaves, prick the fruit with a fork and set them aside.

Heat the vinegar, sugar, cloves and peppercorns in a small
saucepan over a low heat and stir to help the sugar to dissolve.
Once the sugar has dissolved, add the damsons and poach them for
three minutes, bobbling in the syrup, until tender but still holding
their shape. Remove the damsons from the heat and let them soak
up the liquor overnight.

In the morning sterilise a jar – just wash it, then place in the oven
for ten minutes at 80°C/gas ¼ to dry.

Put the pan back on the heat and bring to the boil once more. Using
a slotted spoon, scoop the damsons into the sterilised jar and leave
the syrup to cool.

When the syrup is cold, pour it into the jar, making sure the damsons
are covered, and screw the lid on firmly. If possible leave for a few
weeks in a cool, dark place before using.

Pork chop & vinegar

A thick, rosy pork chop is a supper that fills me with contentment. When cooking chops, it's important to slowly render the thick fat until it is brown, almost charred, and to crisp the edges. The vinegar cuts through and mellows the fat, adding the perfect amount of piquancy.

Makes two large plates

extra virgin olive oil
50g plain flour
2 large pork chops
1 red onion
a pinch of salt
1 tsp pink peppercorns
50ml red wine vinegar
100ml chicken stock
2 tbsp double cream
50g butter

Preheat the oven to 200°C/gas 7.

Heat a glug of olive oil in a heavy-bottomed frying pan over a low heat. Tip the flour onto a plate and stir through salt and pepper to season. Coat each side of the chops and dust off any excess flour.

Prop the chops rind-side down in the frying pan to cook the fatty rind and slowly melt away the fat. After about five minutes, turn the heat up until the pan begins to smoke. Now brown the chops for three minutes on each side. Transfer them to a roasting tin and put in the oven for five minutes until cooked through and tender. Remove from the oven and leave to rest, covered with foil, while you make the sauce.

Peel, halve and thinly slice the onion into half-moons. Heat a little olive oil in another pan, add the onion with a pinch of salt and cook on a low heat for eight minutes until soft. Stir through the pink peppercorns, pour in the vinegar and leave to reduce by half. Stir in the stock and leave to reduce by two-thirds before stirring through the cream and butter.

Stir the resting juices from the chops into the pan, combining everything together, then pour over the warm chops.

Venison, chard & pickled quince

The colours of this dish remind me of walking my dogs in St James's Park in autumn. I dreamt up this combination at Polpetto and it was so popular that prepping three large venison loins a day became routine. The venison is best cooked rare and left to rest.

Makes four large plates

4 x 170g venison fillets
1 large bunch of chard
2 pinches of salt
extra virgin olive oil
1 tbsp butter

For the pickled quince:
1 unwaxed lemon
300ml white wine vinegar
100ml water
150g caster sugar
1 cinnamon stick
3 cloves
1 quince

Start by pickling the quince. Halve the lemon and place it with the white wine vinegar, water, sugar, cinnamon and cloves in a small saucepan. Bring to a gentle simmer and stir a little to encourage the sugar to dissolve. Leave the liquor on a low heat while you peel, halve and core the quince. Cut each one into slivers the thickness of a pound coin and place them in a single layer in a deep tray. Immediately pour over the hot vinegar liquor and cover the tray with tin foil. Leave in a warm place.

Trim any silvery sinew from the fillet pieces and leave the meat on a plate to come to room temperature.

Pour a little water, about 5cm deep, into a pan with a good pinch of salt and set it to boil. Cut the stalks off the chard and set the leaves to one side. Put the stalks straight into the boiling water to cook for a couple of minutes – don't cut the stalks off any earlier as they go black. Drain the stalks and keep the cooking water.

Put a heavy-bottomed frying pan on a medium heat. Rub a little olive oil all over the venison and season it with the other pinch of salt. Carefully place the fillets in the hot pan to cook for five minutes on each side until they are brown all over, including the ends. Remove from the pan, cover with tin foil and leave to rest.

If the venison pan isn't charred, place it back on the heat – otherwise use a fresh pan – and melt the butter until it foams. Add the chard stalks with a spoonful of the water you used to cook them in. Stir the pan to get all the flavour from the bottom where the meat has stuck and add the pickled quince with dash of its liquor. After a minute, scatter in the chard leaves and cook for another minute, just to allow them to wilt. I also like to add the venison's resting juices to the pan.

Put a big spoonful of the chard on each plate, lay a venison fillet whole on top, then spoon a little more of the chard over each before serving.

Clams & sausages

*To me there's nothing better than adding a handful of smooth dappled
clam shells to a smoking hot pan to absorb some meaty, herby juices. I like
to buy Palourde clams, which are found in European waters, from the
British Isles right down to the Mediterranean Sea. They have beautiful
white to soft pink flesh that's ready to eat when the steamed shells pop
open. If you can't find sorrel, use flat-leaf parsley instead.*

Makes four to six small plates

Preheat the oven to 200°C/gas 7.

extra virgin olive oil,
    plus extra
2 garlic cloves
1 red chilli
4 sausages
300g ripe tomatoes
a pinch of salt
1kg clams
125ml white wine
1½ tbsp sherry vinegar
1 tbsp butter
1 bunch of sorrel

Heat a little olive oil in a casserole dish (one that has a lid).

Peel and thinly slice the garlic. Roughly chop the chilli. Run a
knife down the skin of the sausages and squeeze the meat out into
a small bowl.

Halve the tomatoes and wedge them tightly into the dish with the
cut-side up. Pour over two tablespoons of olive oil and scatter in the
garlic and chilli with a pinch of salt. Place the dish uncovered in the
oven to bake for ten minutes, then remove from the oven and crumble
over the sausage meat. Return to the oven for a further ten minutes.

While the tomatoes and sausage meat are cooking, scrub and rub
handfuls of clams together under cold running water. Tap any clams
that are partially open and discard those that do not respond by
closing tightly, along with any broken shells.

Pour the wine and vinegar over the baked tomatoes and sausage
meat, add the clams and dollop over the butter in small lumps.
Pop the lid on the dish and put it back in the oven for ten to fifteen
minutes, or until all the clams open. Give the dish a good shake
after eight minutes to encourage them to open up.

While the clams are baking, run a small knife down the tough sorrel
stems to remove them. Rip the leaves into smaller pieces.

Remove the lid and fold the sorrel and a little more olive oil through
the baked clams. Throw away any that haven't opened.

Spoon into shallow bowls and eat immediately with bread for dipping.

Calves liver in vinegar & red wine with celeriac

A quick and succulent dinner for a cold wintry evening. Many of us have eaten overly bitter liver before, but here the acidity in the red wine vinegar softens its intensity.

Makes two large plates

For the sauce:
1 medium onion
extra virgin olive oil
a pinch of salt
1 garlic clove
2 anchovy fillets
150ml red wine vinegar
250ml Rioja
1 tbsp caster sugar
200ml water

For the celeriac:
1 small celeriac
1 tsp salt
1 bunch of flat-leaf parsley
100ml extra virgin olive oil

For the calves liver:
extra virgin olive oil
2 tbsp plain flour
2 x 120g calves liver

Peel and halve the onion then slice it into half-moon slivers. Pour a little dash of olive oil in a heavy-bottomed pan (one with a lid) and warm over a medium heat. Add the onion slivers with a pinch of salt, then slow cook over a low heat with the lid on for ten to fifteen minutes until they are transparent, but not brown.

While the onions are cooking, peel the garlic and crush with the flat of your knife. Once the onions are cooked, stir through the garlic and anchovies and cook until the garlic has softened and the anchovies have melted.

Pour in the vinegar, bring to the boil and allow the fluid to reduce by half. Add the Rioja, sugar and water and lower the heat. Leave the sauce to simmer for an hour or until reduced by half again.

In the meantime, peel and cut the celeriac into equal-sized chunks. Put the chunks into a large pan and cover with cold water. Add a teaspoon of salt and cook over a medium heat until tender, which will take ten to fifteen minutes. I find the best test to find out whether it is done, is to see if a knife falls through easily.

While the celeriac is cooking, pick and roughly chop the parsley leaves. Drain the celeriac and quickly tip back into the pan. Season while hot, then add the olive oil and parsley. Mash vigorously but leave enough texture so it's not totally smooth. Cover and set aside.

Shortly before you are ready to serve, put a frying pan containing a little olive oil on a high heat. While the pan is heating up, tip the flour onto a plate, season and coat both sides of the liver lightly in the seasoned flour. Lay the liver in the hot pan and cook for about two minutes on each side – no longer as otherwise it will become tough. I think it's nicer to serve the liver a little pink.

As the liver finishes cooking, ladle the sauce over it and let it bubble for the final few moments of cooking time. Serve straight away with the mashed celeriac.

.

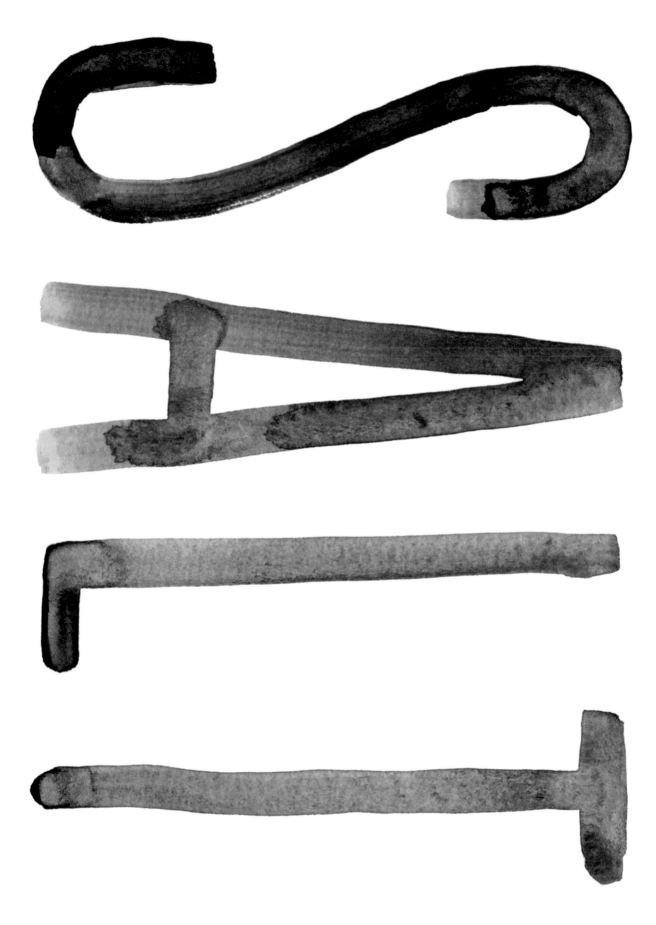

Five

I eat salt on its own, believe it or not. Weirdly, I find it refreshing. I can't help it. I adore it.

More conventionally, there's nothing better than a good pinch of salt and a splosh of extra virgin olive oil on a ripe tomato. It's the simplest way to enjoy food.

Salt has been used for centuries to cure and preserve, to season, to bake and generally to enhance the flavour of almost anything we eat. Like all things, it's a question of moderation, and the ability to season well remains the mark of a good chef. Without it, food is often just bland. Salt brings life to both savoury dishes and sweet things too.

The discovery of salt changed the way we eat forever. It's always been much prized and was a valuable trading commodity for thousands of years. It is even said that the Romans sometimes paid their troops with it – certainly the Latin word for salt, 'sal', is where our word salary comes from.

There are three basic types of salt – standard table salt, unrefined sea salt and rock salt. The problem with table salt is that it tends to contain bleaching agents as well as chemicals that are used to stop it clumping.

Most chefs prefer using Maldon salt or similar flaky kinds of sea salt. Maldon is generally favoured because of its relatively mild effect on food, plus you only need to use a small amount. You could argue that it has a distinctive flavour of its own. While it is a good flaky salt and free from artificial additives, Maldon is not cheap.

I find that 'sel gris', sometimes called Celtic salt, is a good alternative. 'Sel gris' is more affordable and contains no chemicals or bleaching agents. It has a slightly moist consistency with large crystals and comes from the Brittany coast. The grey colour comes from the residual minerals that are normally removed during the purification process. Its real brilliance is that, unlike other salts, it actually tends not to absorb blood and other fluids from meat and so is perfect for cooking medium-rare steaks.

'Fleur de sel' (literally flower of salt) is another highly refined sea salt that is in popular use. Like Maldon this has its own very distinctive flavour and is one of the more expensive varieties.

In any case sea salt tastes a great deal better than the mined rock salt. It has a real saline, oceanic taste that comes through in the food.

I first came across rock salt being used in cooking on my first summer holiday to Italy when I was served sea bass encrusted in an igloo of rock salt. I was astonished when the waiter cracked it open to reveal a perfectly cooked fish underneath. It's a cooking technique that I use as often as I can. The rock salt crust creates an impenetrable barrier, sealing in moisture and juices. It may seem like a lot of salt but in fact the salt never encroaches on the food itself. This dome of salt turns out to provide a perfect hybrid between gentle steaming and roasting with the added advantage of ensuring no loss of flavour.

We've been told salt is bad for us because of its excessive use in the processed food industry. Admittedly it can have a poor effect on our health when we eat too much of it but salt is the original spice. It can make or break a dish: too little and the food is insipid and lifeless; too much and it masks every other flavour. As with most things, when used in moderation salt does nothing but good.

I have learned to appreciate salt's medicinal qualities too. I often become dehydrated when working in a hot kitchen, but a glass of salty water with lemon always seems to do the trick. Also, salt can be used to treat burns, as it draws out the moisture. I wouldn't recommend it because it hurts like hell – my crew think I'm nuts – but for me it beats other more conventional treatments.

Salt is central to life itself. Your body needs it.

Salt cod, tomato & agretti

Wispy and grass-like, agretti (also known as Monk's Beard) has a short season in late spring, but is well worth tracking down. Finding this Mediterranean succulent will give you time to soak the salt cod, as it needs a few days to be transformed from a crystalline hunk to the very succulent plump chunks that make this dish so special – using salt cod rather than fresh fish gives the dish more texture and a more intense flavor. The tomato sauce can be made a few days ahead as the taste just improves with time. In fact, you may want to make double the quantity, as it is always very handy to have in the fridge for a quick mid-week spaghetti pomodoro.

Makes four to six small plates

For the salt cod:
500g salt cod
1 onion
1l milk, plus more if needed
2 bay leaves
4 black peppercorns

For the sauce:
1 onion
3 tbsp extra virgin olive oil,
　　plus a dash
a good pinch of salt
2 garlic cloves
a pinch of dried chilli
3 sprigs of thyme
3 sprigs of oregano
2 x 400g tin of plum tomatoes
zest of 1 unwaxed lemon

extra virgin olive oil
1 large bunch of agretti

Rinse the cod under cold running water until there are no salt crystals left on it. Place in a large container, totally immerse in cold water, cover and leave in the fridge overnight to soak.

In the morning discard the water, gently rinse the fish, cover with fresh cold water and put it back in the fridge (covered) to repeat the overnight soaking process. Once you've done this a couple of times so that fish has been soaked for a minimum of thirty hours overall, it should be ready to cook. It is best to check at this stage that the soaked fish hasn't retained too much salt – I run my finger along it and then lick my finger to check the saltiness.

To make the sauce, peel, halve and slice the onion into half-moon slivers. Put the olive oil in a heavy-bottomed pan over a medium heat and stir through the onions with the salt. While onions are cooking, peel and finely slice the garlic.

Check the onions after ten to fifteen minutes. Once they are soft with a little colour, stir through the garlic, chilli and sprigs of herbs. After another minute or so, add the tomatoes and their juices (rinse and swill the tins with a tiny bit of water and add this too). Keep the heat high for a few minutes to begin with, avoiding the temptation to keep stirring the pan. Then turn the heat down to a gentle simmer and let the sauce reduce without breaking up the plum tomatoes too much. Remember that the longer you cook it, the better it'll be.

After about thirty minutes the tomatoes should be thick and sticky. Remove the pan from the heat and grate over the lemon zest followed by a dash of olive oil. Check the seasoning and carefully stir to combine everything.

Peel and halve the onion for the cod, then put it in a roasting tray with the milk, bay leaves and peppercorns. Place the tray on the hob over a medium heat and bring the milk up to a gentle simmer.

While the milk is warming up, very gently drain the fish and give it a final rinse. Place the cod in the warm milk. The milk should just cover it, so add a little more if necessary. Reduce the heat to low and cook for about ten minutes until the cod starts to flake.

Remove the cod from the milk with a slotted spoon and peel off the skin, running your finger along the pieces to check for bones. Break the flesh into large, irregular chunks and set aside.

Heat a little olive oil in a large pan, add the agretti and let it wilt over a low heat for a few minutes. Then stir through the tomato sauce and fold through the flaked cod.

Best eaten with focaccia (page 38) to mop up all the juices.

Baccalà mantecato

This dish is the heart and soul of Venice, and the first thing I eat whenever I visit. It can be tricky to get right and requires a lot of hard beating. Daunting? Maybe, but it is particularly rewarding to make and exquisite to eat. It's worth making a large batch and turning any leftovers into salt cod croquettes. You will need to start preparing this dish two or three days before you want to serve it, to allow sufficient time to soak the salt cod (which you should be able to find at specialist delicatessens and Spanish food shops).

Makes nearly half a kilo

500g salt cod
3 garlic cloves
250ml vegetable oil
1 onion
1l milk, plus more if needed
3 bay leaves
3 black peppercorns
1 tbsp double cream (if needed)

Rinse the cod under cold running water until there are no salt crystals left on it. Place in a large container, completely immerse in cold water, cover and leave in the fridge overnight to soak.

In the morning throw the water away, gently rinse the fish, re-cover with cold water and return it (covered) to the fridge to repeat the overnight soaking process. Once you've done this a couple of times so that fish has been soaked for a minimum of thirty hours overall, it should be ready to cook. It is best to check at this stage that the soaked fish hasn't retained too much salt. I run my finger along it and then lick my finger to check the saltiness – it should be almost imperceptible.

Peel and bash the garlic with the flat of your knife. Put the oil and garlic in a saucepan over the lowest heat on the hob. If you have a diffuser put this underneath too to distribute the heat as evenly as possible across the base of the pan. You want the oil to be kept warm so that it will be infused with the garlic but not to boil, so if any small bubbles start to appear, remove it from the heat for a few minutes before returning. Leave it on the heat to warm and infuse for at least ten minutes while you prepare the other ingredients.

Peel and halve the onion, then put it in a roasting tray with the milk, bay leaves and peppercorns. Place the roasting tray on the hob over a low heat and bring the milk up to a gentle simmer.

While the milk is getting up to a simmer, very gently drain the fish and give it a final rinse. Place the cod in the warm milk. The milk should just cover it, so add a little more if necessary. Raise the temperature slightly to a medium heat and cook for about twenty minutes until the cod starts to flake.

While the fish is cooking, put an ovenproof bowl in the oven at about 150°C/gas 3 to warm up slightly – you don't want it to be scalding hot, but it needs to be above room temperature.

Gently remove the fish from the milk and peel off the skin while the fish is still hot (a pair of clean rubber gloves comes in very handy here). Pick through the fish for any bones, then transfer the flesh to the warm bowl. Strain the warm milk into a jug.

Take a flat-ended rolling pin, or pestle and mortar, and pound the cod flakes for at least ten minutes or so. Dribble in a tiny bit of milk and keep bashing it. Once it has broken down to a sort of wet-hair consistency, dribble in a little of the warm garlic oil, making sure you don't tip in the garlic cloves themselves. Pound the mixture some more. Keep alternating between slowly trickling in the warm oil and bashing the cod. If at any point the mixture looks as though it'll split, bring the tablespoon of cream to boil in a small pan and stir through a few drops while it's still hot. This helps to stabilise the process.

Eventually you'll have a thick glistening paste. Taste it to check the seasoning. Depending on how long you've soaked the cod it may or may not need salt. It is now ready to serve at room temperature with a few slices of baguette and a grind of black pepper. Baccalà is best eaten immediately, but any left over will keep in an airtight container in the fridge for a day or two.

Blackberry & Pastis sea trout

Aniseed works especially well with fish, and it's a combination I've always been fond of. The French liqueur Pastis replaces the more conventional use of fennel here, adding depth of flavour. Maldon sea salt or ground rock salt works particularly well for marinating the fish, while the blackberries add sweetness and turn the trout a vibrant deep purple. I like to eat this thinly sliced on slightly toasted rye bread.

Serves four as a nibble

170g blackberries
3 tbsp salt
1 tbsp Muscovado sugar
1 tbsp Pastis
zest of 1 unwaxed lemon
1 sea trout, gutted
*   and butterflied*

Put the blackberries in a bowl and mash them into the salt, sugar and Pastis. Zest over the lemon and stir through the mixture. Smear it generously over the fish, wrap in cling film and leave in the fridge overnight.

In the morning, rinse off the marinade under cold running water and pat the fillets dry.

Bring the fish to room temperature and slice to serve on warm toast.

Wrap any uneaten trout in cling film and store in the fridge for up to a week.

Celeriac & prosciutto

Don't be intimidated by the ugly celeriac. It's not a pretty vegetable but it is one that I get excited about every autumn. The salt is crucial here, working to soften the vegetable's hard unruly edge. I always use Maldon sea salt for this. My favourite prosciutto is San Daniele. It's more delicately cured and meaty than most others, and above all I prefer the texture.

Makes four small plates

1 small celeriac
juice of 1 unwaxed lemon
a very generous pinch of salt
2 heaped tbsp crème fraiche
4 basil leaves
8 slices of prosciutto
extra virgin olive oil

Peel the celeriac with a paring knife, then quarter into manageable pieces and cut into very thin slices either by hand or on a mandolin. Layer the slices on top of each other like a pack of cards, cut into matchsticks and place them in a bowl.

Squeeze over the lemon juice, sprinkle on the salt and run your fingers through the celeriac to coat it all. The sticks will still feel very hard at this point, but the lemon juice and salt will break them down.

Leave the celeriac to soften for at least fifteen minutes – if you want to get ahead, you can prepare this up to a couple of hours before serving.

When you're ready to serve, drain most of liquid away, then fold through the crème fraiche. Tear the basil leaves and fold them through too.

Spoon a little of the creamy celeriac onto each plate and drape over the prosciutto slices, adding a dash of olive oil to finish.

Cured duck, lentils & roasted grapes

I don't think people use home-curing enough any more, despite how simple it is. I like to use Maldon sea salt or ground rock salt when curing. This dish requires a bit of advance planning as the meat needs three to four days to cure. It hangs in the fridge looking like Christmas crackers, and for me the taste of the cured duck rivals the finest bresaola.

Makes six small plates

For the cured duck:
2 duck breasts
50g salt
1 tsp caster sugar
3 sprigs of thyme

For the lentils:
450g Puy lentils
1 bay leaf
1l chicken or vegetable stock

For the roasted grapes:
1 bunch of seedless red grapes
2 tbsp runny honey
extra virgin olive oil
4 sprigs of thyme
a pinch of salt

1 small bunch of
*   flat-leaf parsley*
extra virgin olive oil
1 unwaxed lemon

Score the fat on the duck breasts diagonally. Combine the salt, sugar and thyme sprigs in a container, then put half of it aside in a separate bowl. Put the duck breasts in the container and rub thoroughly with the mixture. Lay the duck breasts on top of the other half of the herbed sugar-salt in the bowl. Cover with any remaining mixture from the container. Leave in the fridge covered overnight.

In the morning, take the duck out of the fridge and rinse it under cold water. Cut either a piece of muslin or a clean old t-shirt into two rectangles, each about 15cm x 25cm. Roll one duck breast in each piece of cloth and tie the ends with string like a cracker, making sure that the strings at one end of each bag are long enough to hang it by. Wedge the longer strings underneath a heavy jar or bowl in the fridge and let the bags dangle down. Leave the duck breasts to hang in the fridge for two to three days to cure, after which time the meat will be firm, dry and slightly darker than before.

When you're ready to make the dish, preheat the oven to 180°C/gas 6.

Put the lentils, bay leaf and stock in a pan, bring to the boil and simmer for twenty minutes. Remove from the heat and season while warm.

Scatter the grapes on a baking tray and dribble over the honey, a little olive oil, the picked thyme leaves and the salt. Bake them for thirty minutes until they've burst and are slightly sticky.

While the grapes are roasting, remove the duck from the fridge, unwrap and slice it thinly. Pick and chop the parsley leaves.

Use a slotted spoon to drain the excess liquid from the warm lentils and put them in a large bowl. Mix through the parsley, grapes and sliced duck. Finally, stir through a little olive oil, zest in the lemon, squeeze in its juice and season it to taste. Serve onto small plates.

Treacle mackerel

There are plenty of robust flavours in this, but because mackerel is such an oily fish it can handle them. I have this treacle-cured mackerel on a bit of rye bread as a 'smackerel' before Christmas lunch, or with a poached egg and a little handful of watercress as a light meal.

Makes enough for four people
(or one greedy bear)

1 tsp fennel seeds
2 tsp black treacle
1 tsp wholegrain mustard
2 tbsp Maldon sea salt or
ground rock salt
2 tbsp runny honey
2 whole mackerel, butterflied
and pin-boned

Toast the fennel seeds in a dry pan for a minute or two.

Melt the treacle in a small saucepan over a low heat. Remove from the heat and stir through the mustard, salt, honey and fennel seeds. Spread the mixture over the topside of the two pieces of mackerel. Put the fish in an airtight container and leave in the fridge overnight to cure.

Bring to room temperature and slice before serving.

Roasted celeriac with sage & garlic

I love this knobbly winter vegetable. Roasting it with a little garlic and sage makes a great alternative to boring old potato wedges.

Makes four to six portions

1 celeriac
6 garlic cloves
8 sage leaves
4 tbsp extra virgin olive oil
½ tsp salt

Preheat the oven to 220°C/gas 9. Place a roasting tray in the oven to warm up. Place a large pan of water with a generous pinch of salt in it over a high heat and bring to the boil.

While the water is heating up, peel the celeriac with a small knife and slice it into wedges. Leaving the skin on the garlic cloves, bash them with the flat of a knife and tear up the sage leaves.

Scoop the celeriac wedges into the boiling water and reduce the heat to a simmer. Remove and drain the celeriac after six minutes— it should be tender but not fully cooked.

Pour the olive oil into the hot roasting tray, tip in the celeriac, sprinkle with the salt and place in the oven. After fifteen minutes, use a wooden spoon to stir through the sage and garlic.

Roast for a further forty-five minutes until crisp and tender. Best eaten straight from the roasting tray on its own as a snack or as a side to a juicy steak.

Slow-cooked lamb with apples & potatoes

As well as being added to the dish itself, salt can also be used in the cooking process to preserve and intensify flavour. Here the salt-dough crust traps the juices, producing the most succulent meat. Plus it is exciting to serve, like opening a long-anticipated present. I like to use Cox apples for this dish but you can use other varieties if you prefer. Similarly, feel free to use wholemeal or plain flour instead of strong flour for the salt dough.

Makes four large plates

For the lamb:
1.6kg boned shoulder of lamb
1 tbsp butter,
*   at room temperature*
3 garlic cloves
3 sprigs of rosemary

For the potatoes and apples:
900g Red Desiree potatoes
salt
4 tbsp extra virgin olive oil
4 sprigs of thyme
4 eating apples

For the dough:
5 medium eggs
500g strong flour, plus extra
300g fine salt
150ml water

Take the lamb out of the fridge to reach room temperature and preheat the oven to 200°C/gas 7. Put a deep roasting tin in the oven to warm up.

Quarter the potatoes and tip them into a pan of cold water with a little salt. Bring them to the boil, then turn down to simmer for six minutes. Drain them, giving them a good shake in the colander to rough them up a little.

Pour the olive oil into the hot roasting tin and tip in the potatoes. Give them a shake to coat them in the oil and sprinkle on a pinch of salt and the thyme sprigs. Roast the potatoes for forty minutes until they are cooked through. The important thing here is to give them a little colour.

To make the dough, separate the eggs. Tip the flour, salt, egg whites and water into a mixer and beat until the dough comes together. Alternatively you can mix the dough by hand. Turn out onto a floured surface and knead for about eight minutes until it is smooth.

Turn the oven down to 150°C/gas 3.

Rub the butter over the lamb. Peel and thinly slice the garlic. Make shallow stabs all over the top of the lamb with a small knife and push a couple of slices of garlic and a small sprig of rosemary into each cut. Season with salt and pepper.

Roll the dough into to a rectangle about a centimetre thick. Put the rosemary-spiked side of the lamb onto the centre of the dough. Brush the edges of the dough with water, then fold the sides up and over the lamb to encase it, pinching the edges together to seal. Place the lamb onto a baking tray, brush the dough with a beaten egg yolk and cook

for three hours. Remove the lamb from the oven and let it rest. While the lamb is resting, turn the oven back up to 200°C/gas 7 and prepare the apples. Leaving their skins on, quarter and core them and mix them in with the potatoes. Return the potatoes and apples to the oven and bake for thirty minutes so that they are all cooked through and golden.

Break open the crust at the table for theatre then discard the hardened dough. Fork the meat onto warmed plates to eat with the sticky roasted apples and potatoes.

Buttered pork, cannellini beans & watercress

Pork belly is a cheap flavoursome cut. Don't be put off by the amount of fat; it melts away making the meat incredibly tender, offset by the wholesome lemony beans. Leaving the pork overnight with the salt and sugar begins the curing process, locking in the flavour and tenderising the meat. Curing is a traditional method of preserving food, but now we do it just because it captures the beautiful flavours of even the cheapest cuts. The clarified butter is a nice alternative to goose fat or oil, giving the meat a biscuity richness.

Makes four large plates

1kg pork belly
60g flaky or rock sea salt
30g sugar
2 heads of garlic
1 unwaxed lemon
4 sprigs of thyme
400g dried cannellini beans
1 tsp bicarbonate of soda
1.5–2l chicken or vegetable
   stock
1 onion
1 bay leaf
750g butter
extra virgin olive oil
100g watercress

Cut the pork into large strips, about 6–7cm wide, or ask your butcher to do it for you. Place the pork pieces in a large bowl or airtight container and rub with the salt and sugar.

Slice the garlic head in half horizontally and peel a couple of strips of lemon peel. Add both of these along with the sprigs of thyme to the pork strips, fold through, cover and place in the fridge overnight. Tip the beans and bicarbonate of soda into a bowl, add enough cold water to cover and leave them overnight too (uncovered, to allow them to bubble and swell).

In the morning, rinse the pork under cold water to get rid of the salt, but hold onto the garlic and lemon peel. Pat the meat dry, place it in a roasting tin with the garlic and lemon peel, and set aside.

Drain the soaked beans and rinse them under cold water. Tip them into a saucepan and pour in enough stock to submerge them about two to three centimetres below the surface. Peel and halve the onion and add it with the bay leaf. Cover the saucepan and place over a medium heat until the stock begins to boil. Once it starts to bubble, remove the lid and turn the heat down to simmer very gently.

Preheat the oven to 150°C/gas 3.

Clarify the butter by melting it in a pan over a medium heat until the butter boils and all the milk solids come to the surface. Skim the solids from the top with a ladle.

Pour the clarified butter over the pork, cover the tray with foil and put into the hot oven for three hours.

While the pork cooks, check on the beans: they might need topping up with a little water or stock. Resist seasoning them until they're cooked. Check after they've been simmering for thirty minutes – the beans should be soft and tender. Remove from the heat and while they are still hot, stir through salt and pepper to season and a splash of olive oil.

Rinse the watercress and pick through, removing the stalks and any gnarly bits. Fold the leaves through the beans.

After three hours' cooking, check the pork – you'll know it's ready when it completely falls apart when pulled at with a fork.

Serve the pork in big chunks on top of the beans and wilted watercress.

Baked sea bream
& hispi cabbage

*Making this reminds me of burying my sister in sand on the beach in
Salcombe as a child. You need a whole kilogram of salt to create the
moistest, most delicious, fall-off-the-bone flesh. Bringing the flaming fish
to the table and cracking the salt crust is very theatrical. This dish works
beautifully with the almond mayonnaise on page 203.*

Makes two large plates

1kg rock or grey salt
590g sea bream
1 unwaxed lemon
3 sprigs of oregano
2 tbsp Pernod
extra virgin olive oil

For the cabbage:
1 head of hispi cabbage
25g butter
a pinch of Maldon sea salt

Preheat the oven to 200°C/gas 7.

Mix enough water with the salt to give a wet sand texture. Pour
half onto the bottom of a shallow tray to create a salt base, then lay
the fish on its salty bed. Roughly slice the lemon and stuff the slices
into the cavity of the fish along with the oregano sprigs. Then cover
the fish with the remaining half of the salt. Obviously you don't need
to season it, given that it is covered in salt. Pat the salt tightly around
the fish, put in the oven and bake for twenty minutes.

Once the fish has been cooking for about ten minutes, prepare
the cabbage. Put a pan of water on to boil. Remove and discard the
outer leaves, then halve the cabbage head. Separate the individual
leaves and trim away the hard centre stalks. Throw the leaves into
the boiling water and cook for three minutes until tender. Drain the
cabbage, add the butter and salt, and stir amongst the leaves.

Take the fish out of the oven. Pour the Pernod into a small saucepan,
tilting it to the hob flame so that the alcohol catches light (if you
don't have a gas hob, use a long match to set it alight). While still
alight, pour the Pernod over the fish and carefully take it, flaming,
to the table.

Break the salt, which should come off in one great chunk. Scrape the
skin from the fish and, using a small knife, carefully remove the fillets.

Devour with the warm buttery cabbage and a dash of olive oil.

Shortbread

There are so many versions of shortbread. I've been making this one for years. It's the proper fat-fingered variety. Extra buttery and short, and the salt makes it incredibly moreish.

Makes twelve fat fingers

265g unsalted butter
100g caster sugar, plus extra
225g plain flour
60g rice flour
flaky sea salt

Preheat the oven to 160°C/gas 4. Butter and line a 20cm x 20cm baking tray (at least 2.5cm deep).

Beat together the butter, sugar, flours and a generous pinch of flaky sea salt in a mixer or by hand in a large bowl until the dough comes together.

Scrape the dough into the tray, place a piece of baking paper over the top and firmly push the dough down. Run your hand over the surface until it is even and smooth, spreading the dough right into the corners, then remove the baking paper. Use a fork to prick small holes lightly all over the surface of the dough. Place the tray in the freezer for ten minutes – this helps the dough to relax and stops it from becoming too greasy.

Put the tray straight into the oven from the freezer and bake the shortbread for thirty minutes until the edges are slightly browned and the top is golden.

When it comes out of the oven, score the shortbread into fingers and scatter over some extra caster sugar and a couple of pinches of flaky salt. Leave to cool in the tin.

Once it is completely cool, slice down the score marks and eat – or store in an airtight tin for a couple of days, if you can resist eating it all at once.

Bay salted caramel

I salivate every time I make this and find it hard not to dip my finger in the hot mixture. Glossy, lava-like caramel sludge, this is best eaten warm, poured over some plain vanilla ice cream.

Serves eight

150g butter
150g Muscovado sugar
4 fresh bay leaves
5g flaky sea salt
150g double cream
50g dark chocolate

Place the butter in a saucepan over a low heat. Once it's melted, add the sugar and stir until it has dissolved. Add the bay leaves and leave to simmer for a couple of minutes. Stir in the salt.

Take the pan off the heat and carefully pour in the cream. It might splutter and spit when you do this, so take care. Whisk until the mixture is thick and glossy. Break in the chocolate and stir until completely combined.

Allow it to cool slightly before eating.

Six

Fish and chips, bacon butties and hamburgers demand a good slug of tomato ketchup. It's both the sweet, slightly acidic taste and the vibrant blood-red colour that complements these foods so well.

I, like so many other people, have many happy childhood memories of this crimson condiment in its iconic narrow-topped glass bottle. It's just so satisfying: the way it pours so generously when new, but then later needs crafty persuasion to get it out – a strategically placed butter-knife, a sharp tap on the table or a serious wallop – the lengthier the process of extraction, the more you want it out.

Even so, there's a time and a place for it. There's something quite naughty about requesting ketchup in a fancy restaurant. I've never done it myself but I've seen people do it and it rarely goes down well. Personally I would be more than slightly peeved if someone smothered the zucchini fries I'd just prepared with it.

The original ketchup seems to have its origins in the Far East, as some kind of fermented fish sauce popular long before tomatoes were added to the mix. Early recipes for it have been around since the eighteenth century, as well as early versions involving mushrooms as the main ingredient.

Aside from culinary applications, I myself have found other more practical uses for it; I apply a thick layer to clean copper pans, for instance, which sounds odd but actually makes them look brand new. I also remember using ketchup on my sister's hair. She was white-blonde and her hair would turn green after swimming in a chlorinated pool – easily remedied by covering it for an hour or so in ketchup. To be honest I'm not sure my sister was ever quite as keen as I was to repeat this experiment!

There's a bottle of tomato ketchup lurking in most people's cupboards or fridges, so it makes sense to find new and innovative uses for it. In truth, there's more to it than just a condiment.

Making your own ketchup is great fun and a great way to use up any tomatoes or passata you have left over. Homemade ketchup isn't necessarily better than shop-bought. To be honest, it's not really a fair comparison as there's a world of difference between the two. All the classic recipes for ketchup require a lengthy process of cooking and simmering but it is possible to make a quick version too. In fact the original bottled kind is actually a very simple mixture of tomato paste, corn syrup, vinegar, sugar and seasonings. If you decide to make your own ketchup, you'll find that it's just not as sweet as the gloopy condiment we know and love. The end result will be closer to chutney. Nevertheless it's very satisfying to see a row of beautiful red bottles lining the shelves, and the cooking process fills the kitchen with the delightful smell of tomatoes and spices.

There is a reason why this sauce remains so popular. Over the years the manufacturer has managed to create just the right balance of tangy sweetness and tomatoey fruitiness. It provides that perfect 'ketchup' flavour without being too overpowering.

It can be challenging to cook with, but the outcome more than makes up for it. Don't be afraid to get imaginative with ketchup.

Brown shrimp, kohlrabi & apple

This is my take on the classic prawn cocktail. I love kohlrabi and, if you haven't discovered it already, I think you might too. It can look a little alien with its greeny-purple tinge, bulbous and gnarly shape and large leafy stems poking out the top. Often thought of as a winter vegetable, it's actually best in the summer when it's the size of a small fist, with the crunch of an apple and a refreshing mild watery taste. It adds a clean flavour and texture here, which balances out the strong ketchup. I like to make this with crunchy sweet Pink Lady apples, but feel free to use other varieties.

Makes four small plates

1 tsp caraway seeds
1 unwaxed lemon
1 small kohlrabi
1 eating apple
a pinch of salt
1 tsp ketchup
1 tbsp crème fraiche
100g brown shrimp
extra virgin olive oil

Toast the seeds in a hot pan for a minute or two until they smell fragrant. Set aside to cool. Zest the lemon, then halve and squeeze the juice.

Peel the kohlrabi and slice it very, very thinly into disks on a mandolin or carefully by hand. Slice the whole, unpeeled, cored apple, cutting it horizontally through the middle to give you very thin hoops. Place the apple and kohlrabi in a bowl with the lemon juice and salt; this will stop them from browning as well as helping to soften and break down the kohlrabi.

In a small bowl, mix the ketchup, crème fraiche, shrimps and caraway seeds, then gently fold through the apple and kohlrabi slices.

Add salt and pepper to taste and dress with the lemon zest and a splash of olive oil before serving.

Baked crab & ketchup

This is actually a kind of soufflé, but don't let that put you off. It's not a classic soufflé anyway, because you bake it in a water bath, and it doesn't rise much. The ketchup adds a spicy, almost devilled crab taste. It's satisfyingly rich and always a crowd-pleaser.

Makes four small plates

butter, to grease
flour, to line

For the baked crab:
40g Parmesan
20g mild Cheddar
50g butter
25g plain flour
170ml milk
1½ tbsp ketchup
a few drops of
    Worcestershire sauce
a dash of Tabasco sauce
a pinch of Cayenne pepper
2 eggs, separated
100g brown crabmeat
a pinch of salt
a pinch of black pepper

For the sauce:
275g baby plum tomatoes
1 garlic clove
50g butter
2 tbsp crème fraiche
4 basil leaves
1 unwaxed lemon

Preheat the oven to 170°C/gas 5. Butter and lightly flour four medium-sized ramekins, tapping out any excess flour. Grate the cheeses on a coarse setting and set aside for later.

In a small saucepan melt the butter until it bubbles and froths, then add the flour and stir, stir, stir. Cook the flour and butter paste for three minutes then trickle in the milk gradually, stirring vigorously, and cook for a further three minutes, continuing to stir until the mixture becomes smooth and thick enough to coat the back of a spoon.

Put the cheeses, ketchup, Worcestershire sauce, Tabasco, Cayenne, egg yolks, crabmeat and a pinch of salt and pepper in a bowl, then fold through the warm Béchamel sauce. Cover the mixture with cling film directly on the surface (to stop a skin forming) and place in the fridge to cool.

While the crab mixture is cooling, whisk the egg whites in a clean bowl to soft peaks; once you can draw a ribbon-like strip over the surface, they are ready.

Dollop a spoonful of the fluffy whites into the chilled crab mixture to help loosen it then carefully fold the rest through, drawing figures of eight with your spoon. Once there are no white lumps left, spoon the mixture into the ramekins until they are two-thirds full.

Lower the ramekins into a roasting tin and carefully pour in enough tap-warm water to come halfway up their sides. These won't rise enormously on baking, but leave a little space above each one in the oven to allow for some increase in height. Bake for about twelve to fifteen minutes until firm to touch but still with a slight wobble, then leave to stand for five minutes.

While the crab is baking, make the sauce. Bring a pan of water to the boil. Make a small cross on the base of each tomato, gently so as

not to cut through the flesh but deep enough to go through the skin. While waiting for the water to boil, peel and finely slice the garlic and fill a large bowl with cold water, and ice if you have any.

Once the water has reached a rolling boil, add the scored tomatoes for one minute or until the skin pops back, being careful not to overcook them. Use a slotted spoon to remove the tomatoes and lower them into the cold water. Peel the tomatoes and discard the skins, which should come away easily.

Heat the butter in a large heavy-bottomed pan on a medium heat and let it foam, caramelise and almost burn – the butter will smell almost like digestive biscuits at this point. Quickly add the garlic and fry until lightly golden then scatter over the tomatoes, making sure they form a single layer. Spoon the foaming butter over the tomatoes for two minutes, then dollop in the crème fraîche. Swirl the pan so as not to break up the tomatoes – the crème fraîche will melt and bubble. Cook for about five minutes until the tomatoes collapse but still hold their shape, then season to taste, tear over the basil leaves and add a squeeze of lemon juice.

Run a butter knife (or any blunt-ended knife) around the edge of each ramekin and tip the baked crab onto small plates, spooning over the sauce before serving.

Smoked duck, apricot & hazelnuts

This is a punchy dish with lots of big flavours, but it isn't heavy and looks really dainty on the plate – the celery ribbons, the deep-red flesh of the duck breast and the charred, slightly squished plums. I love plating it, getting my hands dirty then letting the food collapse loosely on the plate. Allow roughly five pieces of smoked duck per person.

Makes two small plates

1 tsp ketchup
2 tbsp extra virgin olive oil, plus extra
juice of half a lemon
50g hazelnuts, skin on
1 head of celery
1 packet of smoked duck
2 fresh apricots, ripe
a pinch of salt

Preheat the oven to 180°C/gas 6.

Make the dressing by mixing together the ketchup, olive oil and lemon juice, and season with a little salt and a smidgen of pepper. Set aside until needed.

Toast the hazelnuts on a dry baking tray in the hot oven for three minutes until you can smell a nutty aroma. While the nuts are toasting, place a griddle pan on a medium heat, as you need it to be very hot, almost smoking.

Tip the hot toasted nuts into the centre of a tea towel, wrap it in a bundle so the hazelnuts can't escape and rub the bundle on a table or work surface to get rid the skins. Allow the nuts to cool, then crush using a mortar and pestle and set aside for later.

Remove the outer sticks of celery. Using a peeler, cut long thin ribbons from the centre sticks, and pluck and keep the leaves. Place the ribbons and leaves in a large bowl. Tear the duck into morsels and scatter over, along with the crushed hazelnuts.

Once the griddle is super hot, halve the apricots, drizzle over a drop of olive oil and sprinkle with the salt. Place on the griddle cut-side down. Don't be tempted to move them around, as you want the lovely char lines. Cook the apricots for two to three minutes then remove carefully from the griddle using tongs. When they're cool enough to touch, slice each half into thirds, so you don't get massive chunks that will overpower everything else.

Pop them into the bowl with the celery, duck and nuts. Trickle over the ketchup dressing and fold through with your hands. Taste for seasoning then scatter over plates to serve.

Mackerel paste with pickled gooseberries

Smoked mackerel is an ideal partner to balance ketchup, as its creamy moist fillets are bold enough to stand up to the strength of the sauce. There are many types of smoked mackerel and it's best to avoid the coated, vacuum-packed varieties in favour of fillets bought from a farmers' market or good food hall. This mackerel paste can be rustled up in no time and is perfect on crusty sourdough. I often pickle gooseberries the day before, to give the flavours time to soften.

Makes four small plates

For the pickled gooseberries:
250g gooseberries
100ml white wine vinegar
25ml water
75g caster sugar
1 cinnamon stick

For the mackerel paste:
300g smoked mackerel,
   skinned and boned
5 anchovy fillets, finely chopped
100g butter,
   at room temperature
2 tsp ketchup
1 tbsp creamed horseradish
black pepper, to taste

4 slices of sourdough

Begin with the gooseberries as they need time to mellow. Top and tail the fruit. Combine the vinegar, water, sugar and cinnamon in a small pan over a low heat, stirring to help the sugar dissolve. Once the sugar has dissolved, add the gooseberries and poach them for ten minutes until they collapse and pop in the syrup. Place a small plate on top of the gooseberries to stop them bobbing up for first five minutes. Then take the plate off and turn up the heat to drive out all the liquid. Don't be tempted to stir too much – you want to retain some of the original shape of the fruit.

Pour off any excess liquor, as the gooseberries will weep out a lot of liquid during the cooking process, continuing to reduce the mixture till it's a lumpy jam-like texture. Remove from the heat, spoon the gooseberries into a bowl to cool down and then chill completely in the fridge. If possible, leave them there overnight to allow the flavours to soften.

Remove any skin left on the mackerel and flake the flesh, running your fingers through to pick out any bones. Place the mackerel and anchovies in a mortar and use the pestle to pound them until the mixture looks like hair you'd pull from the plughole. Pick out any bigger bits of hard outer skin that remain.

Pound in the butter a little at a time until the mixture forms a coarse paste, then stir through the ketchup, horseradish and pepper and taste to check the seasoning.

Spread straight onto toasted sourdough and serve with the pickled gooseberries. You can also pot the mackerel paste in sterilised jars sealed with clarified butter, which will keep for three days in the fridge, as will the gooseberries in their juices.

Brown crab & courgette trofie

I don't normally cook with brown crab because it's so intensely crabby, but it works really well with ketchup. The crabmeat melts away to make a thick, intense, buttery sauce that coats each and every strand of the pasta.

Makes two small plates

100g brown crabmeat
2 tsp ketchup
1 small red chilli
1 courgette
150g trofie pasta
100g butter
extra virgin olive oil
1 unwaxed lemon

First put the water on for the pasta in a big pan with a generous pinch of salt.

While the water's heating up, place the brown crabmeat in a bowl and mix through the ketchup. De-seed and finely dice the chilli. Use a peeler to cut long thin ribbons of courgette.

Cook the pasta for ten minutes until it's al dente, then drain, reserving the water. It is better to undercook the pasta, rather than letting it turn to mush, as it will finish cooking in the sauce.

Place a wide saucepan over a medium heat and add the butter. When it starts to bubble and froth, add the chilli and cook for a minute. Add a ladleful of pasta water to form the sauce. Fold the pasta in to combine. Stir through the crabmeat, the courgette ribbons and a glug of olive oil. If it's looking too gloopy, add a little more pasta water to loosen the sauce.

Finally, zest over the lemon, then halve it and squeeze over some of the juice to taste. Bring everything together in the pan by flipping and shaking it. Taste for seasoning and serve immediately, dividing between two shallow bowls.

Baked ricotta & onion sandwich

My take on a cheese sandwich. It's incredibly easy to make and the topping literally melts as you eat it. Just be patient and let it cool down a little before taking a mouthful, as the onions stay hot blanketed under the warm ricotta.

Serves six as 'elevenes'

50g Parmesan
175g ricotta
1 medium egg
1 medium egg yolk
4 tsp double cream
2 onions
2 tbsp extra virgin olive oil
a good pinch of salt
chicken stock or water
  (if needed)
1 tbsp ketchup
4 thick slices of sourdough

Preheat the oven to 180°C/gas 6.

Grate the Parmesan finely. In a bowl, beat the ricotta until fluffy then fold though the Parmesan, egg, egg yolk and cream. Season with salt and pepper then cover and place in the fridge.

Peel, halve and slice the onions into half-moon slivers. Place a heavy-bottomed pan on a low heat and add the oil and onions, along with a good pinch of salt to help break them down. Place the lid on and leave them to sweat for eight minutes. If they look like they're going to catch or burn at any point, add a splash of stock or water.

Remove the lid and caramelise the onions for another five to eight minutes on a low heat until they're soft enough to squidge between your fingers and have turned a deep caramel colour. Stir the ketchup through the onions and remove from the heat.

Toast the sourdough. Smother each slice with onions and smear over the ricotta – this might be a bit tricky but persevere.

Grill on a high heat for a few minutes until the cheese has melted and is bubbling, then serve straight away. I like to eat this with lightly-dressed leaves.

Marmalade-roasted chicken legs & squash

A great cupboard-raider recipe that makes the leg meat sticky and gunky. Best eaten with your hands. The ketchup binds the dish, giving the chicken a distinctive coral-coloured skin.

Makes four large plates

800g butternut squash
2 tsp coriander seeds
½ tsp dried chilli
2 tbsp chicken stock (or water)
salt
pepper
extra virgin olive oil
100g Muscovado sugar
4 chicken legs, skin on
2 tbsp thick-cut marmalade
1 tbsp ketchup
2 tsp sunflower oil
2 garlic cloves
natural yoghurt, to serve

Preheat the oven to 200°C/gas 7.

Prepare the butternut squash. I always cut the top cylindrical part off the squash and peel it first, then peel and de-seed the rest, but however you want to do it, peel and de-seed it.

Cut the squash into even-sized slices roughly the thickness of a pound coin, and place them in a roasting tray with the coriander seeds, dried chilli, chicken stock, a hefty pinch of salt and pepper, a glug of olive oil and a sprinkle of the sugar.

In a separate roasting tray, rub the chicken legs with the rest of the sugar and the marmalade, ketchup and sunflower oil. Bash the garlic cloves with the flat of your knife, remove the skin and fold through the sticky chicken mixture along with a pinch of salt and pepper, combining everything well.

Place both roasting trays in the oven. Glaze the chicken every ten minutes or so. After thirty to forty minutes, remove the chicken, cover it with foil and leave it to rest on the side while the butternut squash finishes cooking for another five minutes.

Once the squash is cooked through and caramelised, scoop a third of it into a bowl, add a splash of olive oil and use a fork to squish the squash. Fold this back through the caramelised pieces.

Spoon portions of the butternut squash onto plates, topping each with a sticky chicken leg and a spoonful of tart yoghurt.

Braised prawns, fennel & pangrattato

This is a fragrant broth, the type you'd eat on a hot summer's evening, because it's not heavy at all. It's well balanced, with background notes of chilli and aniseed. Best cooked in a casserole dish so that you have a lid to lock in all the flavours. The juices are too good to waste, which makes it ideal for bread dipping. If you have any leftover pangrattato (known as 'poor man's Parmesan'), it's wonderful cascaded over roasted squash or even plain spaghetti for added crunch and texture.

Makes four large plates

For the prawns and fennel:
28 raw prawns
2 bulbs of fennel
50g butter
1 tsp fennel seeds
2 garlic cloves
1 tsp dried chilli flakes
2 tsp ketchup
1 tbsp Pastis
400ml fish stock
3 ripe plum tomatoes
1 handful of flat-leaf parsley
12 Kalamata olives, pitted
extra virgin olive oil
1 unwaxed lemon, in wedges

For the pangrattato:
1 long red chilli
1 garlic clove
a pinch of salt
2 sprigs of oregano
100g stale bread
2 tbsp extra virgin olive oil
zest of 1 unwaxed lemon

Halve the chilli for the pangrattato lengthways and roughly dice, removing the seeds if you don't like too much heat. Peel the garlic and crush to a fine paste with a good pinch of salt using a mortar and pestle. Pick the oregano off the stalks and roughly chop the leaves. Set aside for later.

Tear the bread into large pieces and wedge them into a food processor. Pulse until you have coarse crumbs.

Pour the olive oil in a heavy-bottomed pan. Stir through the garlic and chilli and cook for two minutes to mellow the flavours, then fold through the breadcrumbs. Fry the bread in the pan for a couple of minutes, turning the mixture over every so often, until the breadcrumbs are really crisp and golden. Zest the lemon over the crumbs, scatter over the oregano and season with a little salt and black pepper. Stir everything together, then tip onto kitchen roll to drain.

Prepare the prawns by peeling the shells away from the bodies, leaving the tail part in place. Using a small knife, cut along the back of each prawn and remove the dark vein with the tip of the knife. Cover the prawns and place back in the fridge.

Halve the fennel bulbs and remove the outer layers and very central core, keeping enough of the root to hold the pieces together. Cut the fennel into finger-thick slices and set aside.

Place the butter in a casserole dish (one with a lid) over a low heat. When the butter foams, add the fennel seeds and cook them for a minute before adding the fennel slices. Slowly cook the fennel over the low heat for ten minutes. Once it starts to caramelise, peel and thinly slice the garlic, then add it and the dried chilli to the pan.

Simmer the garlic and chilli in the buttery fennel mixture for a few minutes, then add a splash of water to help soften the fennel so that it doesn't have a hard bite. Stir through the ketchup, Pastis and stock and let it all bubble for five minutes over a high heat.

Halve the tomatoes and scoop out the watery seedy centres. Add the tomato flesh to the casserole and leave to cook for three minutes or until it has wilted a little.

Rinse the parsley under cold water and pat dry, pick off the leaves and roughly chop them. Scatter the prawns, olives and parsley over the fennel broth and stir everything together. Place the lid on and gently simmer on a medium heat for three to four minutes – not much more as there's nothing worse than over-cooked prawns.

Trickle over a little olive oil and season with salt and pepper to taste. Ladle into bowls, dividing the prawns between them, and scatter over the pangrattato before serving with wedges of lemon.

Pork collar in milk & ketchup

This dish might not look particularly beautiful because the milk curdles, the chunks of meat break down, and the ketchup creates a slightly pink tinge. But trust me it's far from a dog's breakfast. Really scrumptious.

Makes four large plates

For the pork collar:
100g butter
4 garlic cloves
1 unwaxed lemon
2 sprigs of rosemary
680g pork collar
1.5l milk
2 tbsp ketchup
⅓ fresh nutmeg, grated
a pinch of ground allspice

For the crumb:
100g piece of stale bread
1 tbsp extra virgin olive oil
a pinch of salt
4 sprigs of thyme
zest of 1 unwaxed lemon

Heat the butter in a large heavy-bottomed pot. Peel the garlic and wallop with the flat of your knife. Use a peeler to remove all the lemon peel in strips. Once the butter begins to foam, add the garlic, rosemary and lemon peel.

As soon as the buttery mixture turns slightly darker, add the pork collar to the pan to brown. Pour over the milk, stir through the ketchup, nutmeg and allspice and make sure that the meat is totally submerged. Bring the milk to the boil and then simmer it on the lowest heat possible for a couple of hours. Cover with a piece of greaseproof paper, pressing it down lightly to make sure the meat doesn't dry out during cooking. The milk will curdle and form small milky bunches, but this is expected so don't panic.

Preheat the oven to 180°C/gas 6.

While the pork is cooking, tear up the bread on a roasting tray, fold through the olive oil and scatter over the salt and picked thyme leaves. Bake for eight minutes until the bread is crisp and golden, then zest over the lemon and set aside.

After two hours the pork will have melted into the milk-ketchup liquor and should collapse at the touch of a fork. Ladle the tender meat and cooking liquor into bowls and top with the crisp crumb.

Ketchup chocolate cake with crème fraiche ice cream

Ketchup gives this a sweet and sour quality that the Italians call 'agrodolce'. A little beetroot goes a long way in baking; it helps to retain moisture and lends an earthy note that balances out the acidity from the ketchup. This is certainly not a light teatime cake as it is rich and dense. The ketchup flavor strengthens over time so it's best to eat this cake immediately. In any case I think it's pretty hard to stop eating it once you've started.

Serves eight

*For the chocolate
ketchup cake:*
400g dark chocolate
250g butter
3 medium eggs
250g caster sugar
300g cooked beetroot
1 tbsp ketchup
150g self-raising flour
a pinch of salt

*For the crème fraiche
ice cream:*
200ml whole milk
150g soft brown sugar
600g full fat crème fraiche
zest of 1 unwaxed orange

Start with the ice cream. Heat the milk and sugar in a pan over a low heat until the sugar has dissolved – this should only take a few minutes. Set aside to cool a little.

In a bowl, mix the crème fraiche, sweetened milk and orange zest together. Pour into an ice cream machine and churn until frozen. Alternatively you can be the ice cream machine: freeze the mixture in a shallow tray for thirty minutes, then remove from the freezer and whisk. Repeat the freezing and whisking process three or four times until the ice cream is smooth and solidified.

Preheat the oven to 180°C/gas 6. Butter and line a 23cm round deep cake tin.

Break up 300g of the chocolate and melt together with the butter in a heatproof bowl over a pan containing a small amount of barely simmering water. While they are melting, stir together the eggs and sugar in a large bowl and grate over the beetroot. Once the chocolate and butter have melted, carefully remove the bowl from the heat and leave the mixture to cool slightly, stirring to combine. While you wait, smash the remaining 100g of chocolate into small pieces.

Stir the ketchup through the slightly cooled buttery chocolate. Pour the chocolate-ketchup mixture into the eggs and fold through the flour, salt and chocolate pieces. Empty the mixture into the prepared tin and place it on the middle shelf of the oven.

Check after twenty minutes – the top should have wrinkled away from the edges and cracked slightly. Bake for another five minutes. Leave to cool in the tin for five minutes before turning out. Slice into slivers and serve each with a ball of the ice cream.

Chocolate pots

For centuries Italians in many regions of Italy, especially Campania and its capital Naples, have enjoyed a rich dessert called 'sanguinaccio'. It is made with a mixture of pig's blood and chocolate and is often served during festivals. This is my version and although it's still incredibly rich, you'll be pleased to hear that it doesn't involve any bloodshed! It's no regular chocolate pot. The ketchup lends a sour, almost berry-like, taste to the richness of the chocolate that is pleasantly unexpected. Make tiny portions as it's so rich you'll only need a little, and feel free to add more chilli if you like it a little 'piccante'.

*Makes four small yoghurt-
   pot-sized portions*

*100ml milk
a big pinch of dried chilli
   flakes
95g dark chocolate, plus extra
150ml double cream
1 tbsp ketchup*

Place a pan on a low heat, pour in the milk and add the chilli. Bring to boiling point, and then remove the pan from the hob and leave to stand for fifteen minutes while the milk infuses and cools.

Break the chocolate into small pieces. Stir the cream into the cooled milk and return the pan to the heat. Bring to boil then add the chocolate and ketchup, stirring through over a low heat until completely dissolved.

Pass the mixture through a fine sieve to remove the chilli flakes, then pour into small cups or glasses. Finally grate a little dark chocolate over each one, cover and leave to chill in the fridge for at least a couple of hours.

Take the chocolate pots out of the fridge twenty minutes before serving to help soften after chilling. I like to eat this with shortbread (page 152) for dipping into the pot.

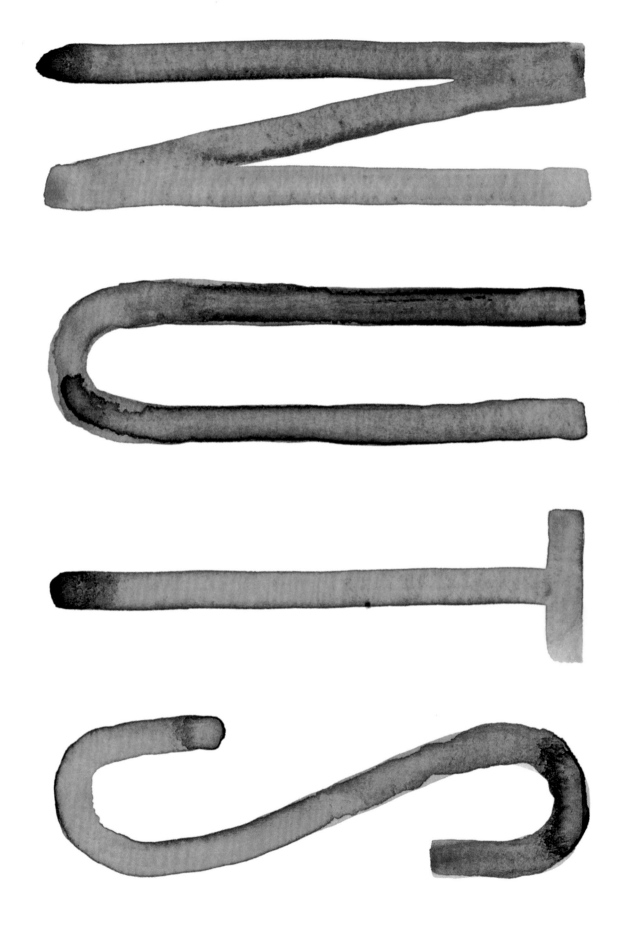

Seven

My kitchen cupboards are full of nuts. I snack on them as the perfect pick-me-up when I'm too busy to sit down or cook a meal. I get really grumpy on an empty stomach so those I love know to have nuts close at hand. They are a perfect snack food as in most cases they come in their own wrapping and hence are often found floating around in the bottom of my handbag.

As a child, I was fascinated by nuts' different shapes and sizes, and repeatedly asked my older siblings to name them for me. Then I would ask my brother Joe to crack them and be enthralled by the differences – the bumpy walnut, the round hazelnut or the smooth almond. The almond is by far the most difficult to crack but the most rewarding to eat, as on chewing it releases a soft milkiness.

We used to gather chestnuts, prickly like hedgehogs, on our dog walks, prise them open when we got home to reveal the nuts in their cosy coats and then roast them. It was a case of Russian roulette on opening the oven door, as a rogue chestnut would often explode.

One of my favourite home-grown nuts is the cobnut, a close sibling to the hazelnut. Unlike most nuts, cobnuts can be eaten while they are young and fresh, straight from their downy shells. They come into season at the end of the summer, ready for early autumn's bounty.

The gnarled walnut is central to Italian kitchens and mine. Walnut in Italian is 'noce', which is the same word for nuts in general, which reflects their importance. Blanching or roasting all nuts, but especially walnuts, will reduce and render the high tannin level in the skins, leaving them less bitter.

Wet walnuts are a real treat as they are available only for a few weeks every autumn. The inside of the nut is 'wet', more damp really, and has a delicate taste in its just-picked state.

Walnuts may be the king, but hazelnuts and almonds are the real culinary nut workhorses that I use in almost every aspect of my cooking. The sweetness of hazelnuts goes superbly with cured meats, fatty pork and bitter leaves and is central to great baking, especially when paired with dark chocolate.

Almonds are the most summery of all the nuts. They have a lighter flavour and almost none of the bitter aftertaste that you can occasionally experience with walnuts and hazelnuts. The subtlety of their flavour means that they are, in many respects, the most versatile culinary nut and can be puréed, powdered, flaked and chopped to make everything from soups to marzipan.

Don't forget the little pine nut. You can improve almost any plain leaves with a few toasted pine kernels dotted through them, or try a scattering over yoghurt.

A trickle of nut oil can beautifully enhance a dish and shouldn't be overlooked either.

I'm certain there is a recipe for every kind of nut. They make unusual and delightful food combinations. Perfect with earthy ingredients from kale to beetroot, slow-cooked lamb, apples, pears and chocolate, as they add texture and a sweet afternote. They have the most natural of flavours and can be complementary to sweet or savoury dishes of every kind.

There are other uses for nuts too. I find that a bundle of warm toasted hazelnuts wrapped in cloth will double as a soothing back rub at work.

Cotechino, pear
& pickled walnuts

I use Opies pickled walnuts for this dish and any good Italian delicatessen should have cotechino out the back – I buy mine from La Camisa on Old Compton Street, one of the oldest delis in Soho. This partially-cooked Italian sausage made from pig's trotters comes from the south of Italy where they are a little less squeamish than their northern compatriots when it comes to cuts of meat. If you have some left over, it's delicious on toast with a little mustard. To get the best from this dish use beautifully ripe pears and don't compromise, as you need their sweetness to balance out the other flavours.

Makes four to six small plates

1 x 250g cotechino
1 x 390g jar pickled walnuts
2 pears, perfectly ripe
extra virgin olive oil to serve

Heat a saucepan of water and then boil the cotechino in the bag that it comes in for fifteen minutes – it should be very tender. Being careful as it will be very hot, cut it from the bag, reserving half the fat. Peel off the sausage skin and discard it. Mash the sausage with a fork – it should have the consistency of chunky mashed potato – then leave it aside to cool.

While it's cooling, slice the pickled walnuts into rounds about the thickness of a pound coin – you don't have to slice all of them, just enough to give you three slivers per portion.

Drain the saucepan and put back on the heat. Halve and core the pears.

Carefully place the cotechino in the hot pan along with the reserved fat – it will spit and splutter so stand back. Mash the fat through the sausage and leave to cook, turning it a little now and then so it starts to crisp up. Then remove the pan from the heat and fold in the pears and walnuts. Don't be tempted to mash it all, just gently turn it to prevent it burning. After a minute, scoop it out onto the plates and pour a tiny splatter of olive oil on each portion before serving.

Roasted beetroot & cobnuts

*I always try to work within the seasons to get the best from my ingredients.
The season for cobnuts and beetroot coincides, but if you can't find cobnuts,
you can use hazelnuts. I make this with beetroots about the size of ping-
pong balls and roast them to intensify their flavour. The cobnuts need little
fuss as they're good enough to eat straight from their shells.*

Makes four small plates

16 small purple beetroots
    with leaves
salt
extra virgin olive oil
1 bunch of thyme
300g shelled cobnuts
100g blanched hazelnuts
zest of 1 unwaxed lemon
2 tbsp red wine vinegar

Preheat the oven to 200°C/gas 7. Cut the leaves from the beetroot
leaving a couple of centimetres of the stems intact. Wash and dry the
good beetroot leaves and put them in the fridge for later.

Scrub the beetroot bulbs under cold running water. Tear sixteen
squares of foil, each large enough to wrap a beetroot in. Place one bulb
in the centre of each square along with a pinch of salt, a drop of olive
oil and a sprig of thyme (setting aside four thyme sprigs to mix with
the nuts), then tightly wrap into individual parcels. Place the beetroot
parcels in a roasting tin with a couple of centimetres of water and bake
for forty-five minutes until tender.

While the beets are cooking, crack open the cobnuts. Dress the cobnuts
and hazelnuts with a dribble of olive oil and a pinch of salt, and toast on
a baking tray in the oven for three minutes until golden. Allow the nuts
to cool then roughly chop or pound them to a very coarse texture. Grate
over the lemon zest and pick and roughly chop four thyme sprigs. Mix
the zest and thyme through the nuts with a pinch of salt.

Unwrap the foil parcels into a large bowl, cover with cling film and
leave for ten minutes; this helps the beetroot skins fall off easily.
Peel them by taking each bulb and pushing your fingers down the
sides to pull down the blackened skin. Discard the skin but keep
any purple liquor.

Add the vinegar, three tablespoons of olive oil and a good pinch of
salt to the beetroot. You can do this up to two days in advance and
the flavours will just improve. Halve any beetroot that are very big,
keeping as much of their natural shape as possible.

Tip the beets into a large pan and warm through over a medium heat
with a tablespoon of their purple liquor. Scatter the leaves into the pan
over the beetroot, gently folding them through so that they wilt a little.
Eat warm with the lemony-herby nuts strewn over the top.

White bean & almond soup

Almond soup is a signature Spanish dish, known as 'ajo blanco'. It's normally served with grapes and always eaten cold. The cannellini beans have little flavour but add a smooth creaminess, which is the ideal counterbalance to the crunch of the ground almonds.

Serves four to six

2 small onions
1 head of celery
extra virgin olive oil
salt
1 bay leaf
2 garlic cloves
200g blanched whole almonds
1 x 400g tin cannellini beans
680ml whole milk
475ml chicken stock
100ml apple juice
150g golden sultanas

Preheat the oven to 180°C/gas 6. Peel, halve and dice the onions and celery (use only the pale central sticks of the celery head).

Heat two tablespoons of olive oil in a heavy-bottomed pan and add the onions along with a pinch of salt and the bay leaf. Gently cook the onions over a low heat until they're soft and break beneath a spoon – this will take about ten minutes. Stir through the celery and the garlic (peeled and bashed with the flat of a knife). Cook gently for about five minutes until they begin to break down, making sure they don't take on any colour.

Put the almonds on a baking tray with a little olive oil and a pinch of salt and toast them for four minutes until golden. Meanwhile drain and rinse the cannellini beans under cold running water. Add the toasted almonds to the onion mixture and cook for a few minutes to allow all the flavours to come together. Empty in the beans and pour over the milk and stock. Simmer on a low heat for twenty minutes.

In the meantime, warm the apple juice in a small pan over a low heat and add the sultanas. Cook gently for five to ten minutes until they are plump and full of apple juice. Remove from the heat and leave to soak up the liquid.

Remove the bay leaf and blitz the soup mixture to a smooth consistency in a blender. Season with a large pinch of salt and a good glug of olive oil to add yet more richness.

Chill until cold and serve scattered with the plump sultanas and a dribble of extra virgin olive oil.

Black pudding, apple & walnuts

My favourite black pudding is the Spanish type they call 'morcilla'. It's more floral and less bloody than the British versions but still beautifully rich, and the sweet caramelised apples and crumbly bitter walnuts provide perfect accompaniments to it. I like the morcilla sold by Brindisa in 350g packets — you'll have quite a lot left over if you make this dish, but I never find it lasts long as it's great first thing in the morning with eggs and bacon or crumbled through tomatoes. If you can't get hold of morcilla, use any good-quality black pudding. Similarly, I love Cox's Orange Pippins in this, but you could use other crisp dessert apples if you prefer.

Makes four small plates

2 dessert apples
3 tbsp icing sugar
25g butter
50g walnuts
extra virgin olive oil
a couple of pinches of salt
150g morcilla

Preheat the oven to 180°C/gas 6.

Peel, core and cut the apples into eighths. Empty the icing sugar into a small pan, so that it thinly covers the base and let it melt over a low heat, patting it with a spatula rather than stirring. Once it has melted and started to darken, tip the apple pieces into the pan, increase to a medium heat and let them begin to caramelise.

After five minutes, add the butter. Cook for a few minutes, turning the apples until the outside of each piece is caramelised — but nor for so long that they turn to mush. Remove the pan from the heat.

Toast the walnuts for a few minutes in the hot oven with a little olive oil and a pinch of salt. Leave to cool.

Cut the morcilla into slices as thick as your little finger. Peel off the skin. Lay the slices on a baking sheet and put them in the oven for a few minutes. While they're warming up, put the grill on medium to high.

Move the morcilla slices to the grill for a couple of minutes to crisp up. Tip the morcilla into the apple pan along with the walnuts and a pinch of salt and toss everything together.

Scatter over the plates and enjoy while it's warm.

Purple kale, shallots & almonds

I've always enjoyed plating this dish. It sums up my approach to cooking – I aim for elegant simplicity. There's something romantic about the mauve frilliness of the purple curly kale in the depths of winter, but if you can't get hold of kale, any tender young green will do well in its place. The stickiness of the slow-cooked shallots binds the dish together, making it incredibly heartwarming. I would always recommend that you buy the almonds with their skins on as they hold much more flavour than the blanched variety. Ultimately it's the almonds that you will remember here.

Makes four small plates

6 *banana shallots*
6 *sprigs of thyme*
extra virgin olive oil
salt
1 *garlic clove*
a pinch of brown sugar
75g *whole almonds*
300g *purple curly kale*
1 *tbsp butter*

Preheat the oven to 180°C/gas 6.

Peel the shallots, carefully removing the root but leaving them whole. Wedge them into a medium pan with the thyme sprigs, two tablespoons of olive oil and a pinch of salt. Cover and place on a low heat for thirty minutes until the shallots have softened and collapsed slightly, but have little colour. While the shallots are cooking, peel and crush the garlic.

Add the garlic and sugar to the shallots. Turn up the heat and cook for ten minutes uncovered, stirring once or twice, until the shallots are sticky and so soft that you can squish them between your fingers.

In the meantime, toast the almonds with a little olive oil and a pinch of salt on a baking tray in the hot oven for three minutes until the natural oils are released and the nuts turn an amber colour. Once cool enough to handle, chop up the almonds roughly.

Wash the kale and cut through the ends of any tougher stalks with a knife to split them. Bring a pan of salted water to the boil and cook the kale for a minute or two – no longer as you want to keep its bite. Drain and set aside.

Warm the butter in a medium-sized pan. When it begins to froth, add the shallots. Top with the kale, stir gently then sprinkle over the almonds and season to taste. Serve immediately.

Castelfranco, prosciutto & hazelnuts

Castelfranco radicchio is often neglected, relegated to being a garnish because it's so pretty with its delicate pink speckles. It's an Italian winter vegetable that is a hybrid between the red-leafed chicory and the endive. The flavour can vary from slightly sweet to agreeably bitter. Here the richness of the hazelnut and the sweetness of the orange help to mellow the leaves with surprisingly satisfying results.

Makes four small plates

75g hazelnuts
1 head of castelfranco radicchio
8 slices of prosciutto, at room temperature

For the dressing:
2 oranges
1 tbsp red wine vinegar
1 tsp honey
a pinch of salt
black pepper, to taste
100ml extra virgin olive oil

Preheat the oven to 180°C/gas 6. Once hot, toast the hazelnuts for a few minutes on a dry baking tray, then set aside to cool. When cool enough to handle, chop roughly.

Tear the castelfranco apart leaf by leaf, breaking up any larger ones and removing any that are damaged. Wash the leaves in cold water and gently pat them dry.

To make the dressing, zest and juice the oranges into a small bowl and add the vinegar, honey, salt and black pepper. Whisk in the olive oil little by little until combined.

Place the hazelnuts, castelfranco and prosciutto in a large bowl and spoon over the dressing sparingly. Fold everything together with a light touch. Have a nibble to check the seasoning.

Divide between the plates and eat straight away.

Dandelion & wet walnut rigatoni

You could call this a variation on a classic pesto. Before I worked in a kitchen the only dandelion I'd come across was the one I fed to the rabbit. Dandelion leaves are best eaten when young, before they get tough. They're especially delicious raw, although the bitterness is an acquired taste, like radicchio. The fresh dewy walnuts, which bind this dish together, are one of the real joys of autumn.

Makes four large plates

50g walnuts
6 bunches of dandelion
100g Parmesan, plus extra
50g butter, plus about 25g
a pinch of salt
a few grinds of black pepper
60ml extra virgin olive oil
20 wet walnuts, to allow
   for duds
500g rigatoni

Put a pan of salted water on to boil. Toast the walnuts for a couple of minutes in a dry pan over a medium heat.

Rinse the dandelion, cut off the roots and discard them. Put a couple of the finer pieces aside to dress the plates later.

When the water has come to the boil, cook the dandelion for three to five minutes until tender. Fish the dandelion out and let it cool slightly, keeping the cooking water. While still hot, roughly chop the leaves.

Put the chopped dandelion into a blender while still warm, add a couple of ladles of the cooking water and blitz it for a moment. Add the walnuts, Parmesan, 50g butter, salt, pepper and olive oil and blitz again. I tend to make the paste quite smooth. Set aside in a bowl and cover it with a piece of cling film.

Put a second pan of water on to heat up. Crack open the wet walnuts, discarding any duds (mouldy ones). Roughly chop and set aside.

When the water has come to the boil, cook the rigatoni for about ten minutes until it is 'al dente'.

While the rigatoni is cooking, put a large pan on the heat with the extra butter. Once the butter starts to bubble, pour in the dandelion paste to warm it through. If the sauce is too thick or it begins to seize, stir in another ladle of the cooking water.

Drain the rigatoni and add it to the sauce, stirring for a minute to make sure the sauce gets into the hollows of the pasta. Serve with a little grated Parmesan over the top, a sprinkling of wet walnuts and the raw dandelion leaves.

Oatmeal & hazelnut mackerel with braised cicorino

Cicorino looks like a beautiful purple or green rose. It's an unusual vegetable, related to chicory (which you could also use) but not as bitter and with less densely-packed leaves. Oatmeal acts as the binding agent here so that the hazelnut can stand out. You can prepare the cicorino up to three days in advance as it keeps well covered in its juices in the fridge.

Makes four large plates

For the mackerel:
50g blanched hazelnuts
75g oatmeal
4 mackerel, filleted
   and pin-boned
50g butter
1 unwaxed lemon, in wedges

For the cicorino:
1 fennel
1 onion
2 tbsp extra virgin olive oil
a pinch of salt
350g cicorino
500ml apple juice, plus more
   (if needed)
500ml vegetable stock
75g butter

Halve the fennel and onion. Cut out the central core of the fennel, keeping enough of the root to hold the pieces together. Slice the onion and fennel in half-moon slivers and put them in a heavy-bottomed pan with the olive oil and a pinch of salt. Cook slowly over a low heat for about ten minutes to soften them without getting colour.

Rinse the cicorino in cold water, removing any damaged leaves. Carefully remove the stalks with a paring knife, keeping the bunches whole, and leave the bunches in a colander to drain.

Once the onion and fennel mixture is soft, add the apple juice, vegetable stock and butter and bring to the boil. Add the cicorino and cook in the liquor for about ten minutes: submerge the leaves, pushing them down with a circle of greaseproof paper topped with a heatproof plate so that the leaves stay submerged in order to wilt and cook evenly.

Taste the liquor, adding more apple juice or salt as necessary to balance out the bitterness of the cicorino, then set aside while you prepare the mackerel.

Preheat the oven to 180°C/gas 6. Toast the hazelnuts on a baking tray for three minutes until the nutty aroma starts to release and the nuts begin to colour. Let them cool for a minute then grind to a medium texture using a mortar and pestle.

Mix the hazelnuts and oatmeal together in a bowl then pour into a shallow baking tray. Press the mackerel fillets firmly into the mixture to coat them all over.

Cook the mackerel fillets two at a time. Melt half the butter in a frying pan on a medium heat until it begins to foam. Once bubbling, put two fillets into the pan so as not to overcrowd it. Cook for two minutes on each side but don't push them around too much as you

want to make sure the crust stays on the fish. Then place them on
a clean baking tray. Melt the rest of the butter in the frying pan and
cook the other two fillets. Then put all of them into the oven for two
minutes to finish cooking.

Ladle out the cicorino into shallow bowls and top with the crisp
mackerel. Serve with lemon wedges and watch the purple liquid turn
pink as you squeeze over the juice.

Almond mayonnaise

A delightful condiment that works especially well with fish and lamb. Toasting the almonds is essential to extract the oil and the maximum flavour. I use a blender or food processor to make this. However, if you don't have one, you can pound the almonds in a mortar and then make the mayonnaise the old-fashioned way with a whisk, a large bowl and a bit of elbow grease.

Makes a small jarful

200g almonds, whole
  and blanched
2 garlic cloves
2 medium egg yolks
250ml extra virgin olive oil
juice of 1 unwaxed lemon

Preheat the oven to 180°C/gas 6. Toast the almonds on a dry baking tray for a couple of minutes, then leave to cool.

Peel the garlic cloves. Tip the cooled almonds and the garlic into the food processor and blitz until they're quite fine. Stir or blitz in the egg yolks.

Keep the food processor whizzing and slowly add the olive oil. If the mixture looks as if it is starting to split, add a little of the lemon juice to loosen it then continue with the olive oil.

Once the oil has been incorporated, slowly add the lemon juice, blitzing all the while. Season with salt and pepper to taste. Stir in a splash of lukewarm water if the mayonnaise seems too thick.

Fresh mayonnaise should be stored in a jar or airtight container in the fridge and eaten within a day or two at the most.

Carrot cake

This is not your everyday carrot cake, as there are a few special ingredients to ensure that it retains its moisture. A lot of shop-bought carrot cakes are too dry and the topping is quite often there just to add wetness. Here the slightly sour and tangy cream cheese cuts through some of the sweetness of the cake.

Serves ten

70g pecans
300g carrots
80g pineapple
2 medium eggs
200g Muscovado sugar
70g desiccated coconut
200g plain flour
1 tsp bicarbonate of soda
2 tsp ground cinnamon
1 tsp mixed spice
½ tsp ground ginger
a pinch of salt
160ml sunflower oil

For the icing:
50g butter
200g icing sugar
100g cream cheese

Preheat the oven to 150°C/gas 3. Grease and line a 23cm loaf tin.

When the oven is hot, toast the pecans on a dry baking tray for a couple of minutes.

Peel and roughly chop the carrots and pineapple. Tip the carrot into a food processor and pulse once or twice then add the pineapple and pecans and whizz for a moment, making sure to retain a coarse texture. You can achieve the same effect chopping everything with a sharp knife but it will take you a little longer.

Whisk the eggs with the brown sugar until they are very fluffy and pale. Stir through the coconut and the chopped pecans, pineapple and carrots. Fold in the flour, bicarbonate of soda, spices, salt and finally the sunflower oil. Pour the mixture into the lined tin and bake for forty-five to fifty minutes until a knife comes out clean. Turn out and cool on wire rack.

While the cake is baking, make the icing. Beat together the butter and icing sugar until it looks like fine breadcrumbs then dollop in the cream cheese and whisk until smooth.

Once the cake is totally cool, ice it and eat it with a nice cup of tea.

Hazelnut chocolate brownies

My brownies are an absolute favourite at home. In fact I've never cooked them in a restaurant but I used to make them for my market stall in Camden Passage in Islington. These brownies have the flaky sugary top, chewy corners and gooey centre that so many recipes don't deliver.

Makes 12 quite big ones

400g darkest chocolate
280g butter
6 medium eggs
450g caster sugar
100g skinless hazelnuts
2 tbsp Nutella
170g plain flour
a pinch of salt
100g chocolate chips

Preheat the oven to 180°C/gas 6. Line a deep 30cm x 20cm baking tray.

Break up the dark chocolate and melt with the butter in a heatproof bowl over a pan of simmering water. Stir to combine then remove from the heat and leave to cool slightly.

In a large bowl, whisk the eggs with the sugar until combined but not yet pale or fluffy

Once the oven is hot, toast the hazelnuts on a dry baking tray for three minutes until they start to smell nutty. Leave to cool, then halve or bash them, leaving them quite chunky.

Pour the chocolate mixture over the eggs and sugar and stir to incorporate. Stir in the Nutella. Fold through the flour with a pinch of salt, then add the hazelnuts and chocolate chips.

Scrape the batter into the tray and bake for ten minutes, then reduce the temperature of the oven to 150°C/gas 3 and keep cooking for about another twenty minutes. By this time the top should look all flaky and cracked and have turned lighter brown, the edges should be wrinkly and the brownie shouldn't be wobbly in the tray. Take it out as soon as it looks like this, as it will keep cooking in the tray as it cools.

Leave in the tin to cool then cut into squares.

Stuffed figs

When you have such a simple pudding, selecting good quality ingredients is key. Buy plump ripe figs and toast and grind your own almonds for the simple frangipane. It will make all the difference.

Makes eight small plates

For the frangipane:
60g blanched whole almonds
60g butter, at room
*   temperature*
60g caster sugar
1 medium egg
zest of 1 unwaxed orange
1 tbsp flour

8 figs
325ml port
*   (or sweet Marsala wine)*
2 tbsp light brown sugar
1 cinnamon stick

Preheat the oven to 200°C/gas 7.

Toast the almonds on a dry baking tray for a couple of minutes until they're aromatic, then leave to cool. Blitz in a food processor or pound them in a mortar until they're quite finely ground.

Cream together the butter and sugar until pale and fluffy. Slowly, slowly dribble in the egg whilst mixing. Stir in the orange zest, flour and almonds. Cover the mixture and put in the fridge to chill for an hour – it has to get cool enough to be able to handle without melting.

While your frangipane is cooling, trim the hard end from the fig stalks, leaving as much stalk as you can, and line a baking tray. Cut a shallow cross into the top of the fig, cutting about a third of the way down, and prise it open slightly, squeezing it a little as you would a hot baked potato.

Roll a large marble-sized ball of the chilled frangipane and wedge it in the top of each fig. Place the figs onto the lined baking tray and bake them in the oven for fifteen to twenty minutes.

Put the port, sugar and cinnamon stick in a small saucepan and place on a low heat, gently persuading the sugar to melt with a stir or two. Once the sugar has dissolved, turn the heat up to medium and reduce the liquor by half, keeping a close eye on it. After ten minutes it should be the consistency of maple syrup and ready to take off the heat.

Arrange the baked figs on plates and pour over the port reduction before serving.

Roasted almond affogato

*There is something very pleasing about the combination of coffee and nuts.
Affogato is traditionally made with simple vanilla ice cream served with
a hot espresso poured over the top. This version is a little more indulgent.*

Serves six to eight

For the praline:
500g almonds
250g icing sugar
100g butter

For the ice cream:
125ml whole milk
750ml double cream
10 medium egg yolks
175g brown sugar

6 shots of espresso, to serve

Preheat the oven to 180°C/gas 6. Lightly oil a baking tray.

Once the oven is hot, spread the almonds on a dry baking tray and
toast them in the oven for a few minutes. Pour them into the oiled
baking tray and set aside to cool.

Tip the icing sugar into a heavy-bottomed pan on a high heat and
gently pat with a spatula to help it dissolve. The sugar will melt
around the edges first; swirl the pan around until the melted sugar is
a deep terracotta colour all over. Remove from the heat and dollop in
the butter. Shake the pan and swirl the mixture again until the butter
has completely melted. Pour the caramel over the almonds on the
oiled tray and leave to cool.

When it's cool enough to handle, tip the praline out of the tray onto
a chopping board and roughly chop it. Divide the praline in half: put
one half in a large bowl to use to flavour the ice cream, and the other
half in an airtight container to sprinkle over when serving.

In another heavy-bottomed pan, warm the milk and cream over
a medium heat to just below boiling point.

In a large bowl, whisk the yolks and sugar until they're light, frothy
and thick enough to hold a ribbon on the surface of the mixture. Pour
the hot milk and cream little by little over the fluffy yolks, stirring
non-stop. Return the mixture to the pan and simmer gently, stirring
constantly to stop the mixture turning into scrambled eggs. When
the mixture is thick enough to coat the back of the spoon – I run my
finger along the back to see that a line stays – it is ready. Remove
from the heat, strain it through a fine sieve over the praline and stir to
combine. Cover with cling film directly on the surface of the custard
so that it doesn't form a skin and chill overnight in the fridge.

In the morning, strain the mixture again, pounding it with a ladle
to squeeze as much of the nutty flavour out of the praline pieces
as possible, discarding the gloopy praline left in sieve. Pour the

strained custard into an ice cream machine and churn until frozen. Alternatively, pour the mixture into a shallow tray and freeze for thirty minutes, then take it out and whisk through before returning it to the freezer. Whisk and refreeze three or four times until smooth and set.

Serve each scoop of ice cream in a small glass with a shot of hot espresso poured over it and some praline pieces sprinkled on the top.

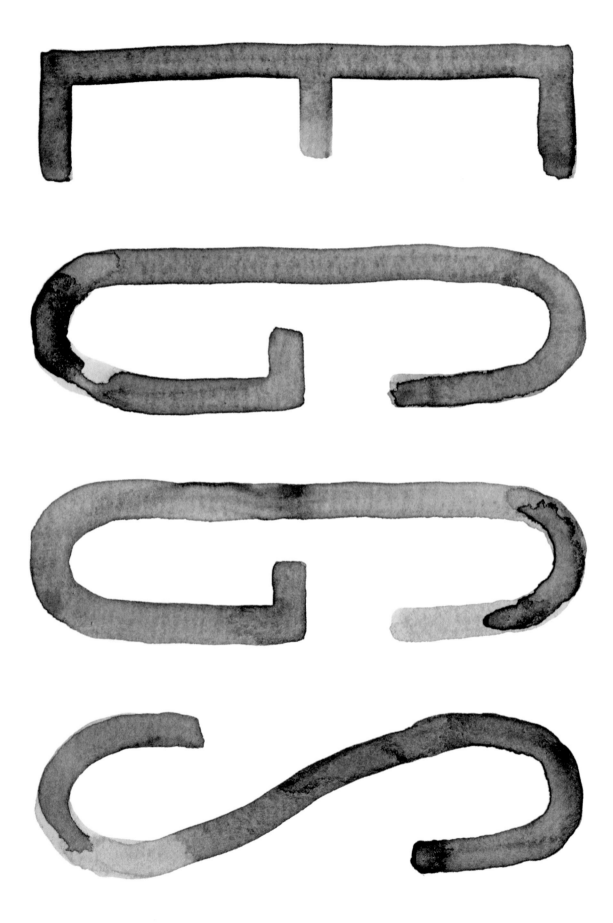

Eight

The best way to know that your egg is fresh is to own the hen that laid it. I was lucky enough to grow up with hens in the garden. We treated them as pets and gave them names; usually television characters of the moment. We knew a lady who would 'hen-nap' battery-kept hens and so we would often receive some poor featherless creatures which were nonetheless great layers. Unlike their miserable existences on a battery farm, their lives with us were long and happy.

Chickens come in many sizes, colours and shapes, from classic run-of-the-mill to daft and frizzy, almost curly, sleek black and everything in between. This has a no real impact on the taste of their eggs. The most important thing is that the chicken has a varied diet, gets to see sunlight and can root around in the ground. This will make for much healthier eggs.

Eggshells vary from deep terracotta brown, sometimes speckled, to pure china white, creamy-hued or even Wedgwood blue. I have often wondered whether there is any difference in taste but in a blind tasting I don't think I could honestly tell.

Burford brown eggs have a wonderful hard, glossy shell that enables them to retain farm freshness and make the most perfect boiled eggs, cakes and custards. White eggs, such as the ones laid by Legbars, have a more delicate shell and are larger with a rich, dense white holding a bold amber yolk, making them best for frying.

From the moment you crack an egg open, you should see from the dark orange yolk that a healthy happy chicken has laid it; the yolk should be bright and stand pert with very little separation from the white. It's hard to keep chickens in Soho, so when I buy eggs I only ever buy the best organic free-range ones.

You can prepare a feast with eggs. They have the ability to transform themselves and the dishes they are added to. When separated, the whites can be beaten stiff to make fantastic meringues or a wondrous puffy soufflé. It is essential that eggs are at room temperature when you are baking or cooking them. At this temperature you will achieve full-volumed soufflés, sponges, mousses and meringues. There really is no need to keep eggs in a fridge.

Without eggs, baking would be practically pointless. They are the base for a great cake or pastry. Eggs enrich with colour, texture and flavour. They help to bind everything together, thicken sauces and glaze pastries and buns.

Eggs have been the cornerstone of the English Breakfast for hundreds of years for a good reason. They retain their freshness easily, they are simple to prepare and until recently they were considered healthy. The health scares relating to eggs are a great pity as eggs contain a whole range of proteins, vitamins and minerals. As with most things, when eaten in moderation eggs are as good for you as we've always believed.

A simple omelette or a soft-boiled egg can often be beyond the abilities of an otherwise accomplished cook. Eggs should not be over-cooked; they are extremely sensitive to heat, requiring a delicate touch.

With some exceptions, they should always be cooked slowly. I even prefer my fried eggs and omelettes slow-cooked. You can take as long as you like with scrambled eggs – they are often treated as a kind of eggy fast food but for best results you need a lot of time and patience. And then, after all the waiting and stirring, the joy of the simplicity of scrambled eggs on hot buttered wholemeal toast with a strong cup of English Breakfast tea. What in the world could be better than that?

Poached egg & truffle

It sounds easy, and it is, but you need to be able to poach a good egg and source the right truffle. The best way to enjoy the highly prized pungent fungi is to keep it simple. Store winter truffles buried in carnaroli rice in an airtight container in the fridge: the truffle will stay fresh and the rice will become beautifully infused, ready to make a perfect risotto. There are a few things you should do once in your life if you can. A trip to Alba, Italy, in October at the height of the white truffle season is one of them. I prefer white truffles to black, but the more plentiful black truffle, with its cracked skin and charcoal marbling, has a gentler smell and taste than its white counterpart. Black truffles are harvested from November to March and, like white truffles, they range in size from a small marble to a large ping-pong ball. You are limited by the seasons and climactic changes when buying truffles, but look for one that is firm and weighty, earthy-smelling and with no soft spots – and always slice on a truffle slicer or with a very sharp knife to get wafer-thin pieces.

Makes two small plates

2 capfuls white wine vinegar
2 medium eggs
1 small white truffle
extra virgin olive oil

Fill a small pan about a third full of cold water and bring it to a rolling boil. Add the vinegar and turn the heat down to a gentle simmer. Crack one of the eggs into a glass or cup.

Swirl the water around in a circular motion. Once the water settles slightly and there a whirlpool effect in the centre, lower the glass or cup into the middle of the swirl so that it almost touches the water and tip the egg out in a quick fluid motion. Lightly poach the egg for three minutes or until the white is just set.

Remove the egg with a slotted spoon and drain on kitchen towel before placing on a plate. Repeat the poaching process with the other egg.

Finely slice a little truffle on the top of each egg, dribble over a little olive oil and season with salt and freshly ground pepper. Serve with bread for mopping up the runny yolk.

Arbroath smokie sformati
& wilted spinach

*Sformati is an Italian soufflé, which I cook gently here in a water-bath.
Unlike French soufflés it won't rise much and is quite dense. An Arbroath
smokie is a smoked haddock from a small fishing village in Scotland
and is still amongst the best-tasting smoked fish you can buy. I like to eat
sformati simply, served with wilted greens or lightly dressed leaves.*

Makes four small plates

butter, for greasing
330g Arbroath smokies
225ml double cream
1 bay leaf
*1 small handful of
    flat-leaf parsley*
2 medium eggs
1 tbsp potato flour
freshly ground nutmeg
zest of 1 unwaxed lemon

For the sauce:
3 tbsp of the cooking cream
200ml white wine
50g butter

For the spinach:
*2 large bunches (about 1kg)
    of spinach*
3 garlic cloves
2 tbsp extra virgin olive oil

Preheat the oven to 180°C/gas 6 and lightly butter the inside of four
155ml dariole moulds.

Lay the Arbroath smokies into a shallow tray, pour over the cream
and add the bay leaf. Make sure the smokies are fully submerged so
that they don't dry out. Bring the cream to the boil over a high heat,
then reduce the heat to a gentle simmer for five minutes until the fish
is tender. Remove the tray from the heat. Remember the smokies
are getting cooked again so they don't have to be cooked through at
this point. Lift the smokies out onto a plate with a slotted spoon and
leave them to cool a little, reserving the cream for later.

While you are waiting for the fish to cool, pick the parsley off the
stems and roughly chop, setting aside for later. Separate the eggs and
whisk the whites in a clean medium-sized bowl until they have a firm
set that holds peaks.

Once they are cool enough to handle, remove the skin and as many
bones as you can from the fish. Flake the chunks into a blender, season
with salt and pepper and pulse until you have a coarse paste. Scrape
the mixture into a large bowl.

Add the yolks to the mixture with a generous tablespoon of the
smokie cream and the potato flour. Stir in the parsley, grate over
nutmeg and lemon zest to taste and fold through the stiff whites with
a figure of eight movement so not to lose any of the air.

Spoon the mixture into the greased moulds. Place them in a roasting
tray and pour boiling water halfway up the sides of tins. Bake in the
oven for fifteen minutes, then leave to stand for five minutes before
turning out.

While the sformati are baking, prepare the sauce and spinach. Place
three tablespoons of the leftover cream in a pan on a low heat and

add the wine. Bring to a gentle simmer until the bubbles get bigger as the sauce thickens, stirring every so often to make sure it doesn't catch. Taste the sauce to check the seasoning – you'll need to be light-handed with the salt as the cream will already be highly seasoned from poaching the smokies. After a few minutes' simmering, dollop in the butter and stir through until the sauce is thick and glossy.

Fill up your sink with cold water and soak the spinach to loosen any sand or dirt. Pull off any thick stems and discard them. Drain the spinach and repeat the rinsing if it still feels sandy. Place the spinach in a colander and set aside to drain off any excess liquid (don't worry about it still being a little wet) while you peel and finely slice the garlic into slivers.

Heat the olive oil in a large pan over a medium heat. Add the garlic and cook for a minute until it is just beginning to brown. Add the spinach to the pan, packing it down a little with your hand if necessary to squeeze it all in. Cover the pan and leave the spinach to wilt for one minute. Lift the lid and use a wooden spoon or tongs to turn the spinach in the pan so that you coat it in the olive oil and garlic. Cover the pan again and cook for another minute.

Remove the pan from the heat and drain any excess liquid by tilting it over the sink, using a wooden spoon to hold back the wilted spinach. Dribble in a little more olive oil and sprinkle with salt to taste (I use a pinch or so).

Divide the wilted spinach between the plates, turn out the Arbroath smokie moulds onto the spinach and spoon over the creamy sauce.

Chickpea, Swiss chard & soft-poached egg

This is wholesome eating at its best. I find it hard to resist piercing the flaxen yolk over the plump pulses. Think of chard as two different vegetables as the stalks need a little more help than the leaves; cooking the stalks with the chickpeas softens their toughness.

Makes six small plates

300g dried chickpeas
3 onions
extra virgin olive oil
1 tsp dried chilli
2 tsp coriander seeds
salt
2 sticks of celery
1 carrot
3 garlic cloves
1 bunch of Swiss chard
1 bay leaf
175ml white wine
1 x 400g tin of plum tomatoes
a splash of malt vinegar
6 medium eggs,
* at room temperature*
black pepper, to taste

Put the chickpeas in a large bowl, cover with cold water and soak overnight.

When you are ready to cook, drain and rinse the chickpeas under cold running water. Place them in a pan and add water until it covers them by about 2.5cm. Peel and halve one onion and add it to the pan with a little olive oil, the chilli and the coriander seeds.

Bring the chickpeas to the boil then reduce the heat and simmer until tender, checking after thirty minutes. Once the chickpeas are cooked remove them from the heat, drain them (reserving the cooking liquor) and season to taste.

Meanwhile peel, halve and dice the remaining two onions. Put the onions in a heavy-bottomed pan with a glug of olive oil and a good pinch of salt, cover with the lid and cook slowly over a low heat for ten minutes, stirring occasionally.

While the onions are cooking, peel, halve and dice the celery and carrot. Submerge the garlic cloves in warm water and leave for a few minutes – this will help the skin to pop off easily. Then cross-chop or use a pestle and mortar to mash the garlic with a good pinch of salt until it becomes paste-like.

Rinse the chard stalks under cold running water and trim the ragged ends. Using a small knife, remove the stalks from the leaves following their natural shape. Roughly chop the stalks into thin strips.

After the onions have been cooking for ten minutes and are soft and tender, stir through the celery, carrot, garlic and chard stalks and add the bay leaf. Stir through and combine and cook for a further fifteen minutes.

Pour over the wine and leave to reduce by half over a medium heat. Add the tomatoes and 300ml of the chickpea cooking liquor followed

by the drained chickpeas. Give the mixture a good stir through and simmer for about twenty minutes until almost all the juices have been absorbed into the chickpeas. Season well while still warm, then fold through the chard leaves and cover with a pan lid to help them wilt into the mixture.

Place a pan of water with a splash of malt vinegar in it over a medium heat and bring to a simmer. Crack one of the eggs into a glass or cup. Swirl the water around in a circular motion and once the water settles slightly and there is a tornado effect in the centre, lower the cup into the middle of the swirl so that it almost touches the water and tip the egg out in a quick fluid motion. Lightly poach for three minutes or until the white is just set. Remove the egg with a slotted spoon and drain on kitchen roll before placing on a plate. Repeat the poaching process with the remaining eggs. If you're confident, poach two at a time.

Ladle the chickpeas into bowls. Place a poached egg on top of each serving of chickpeas and finish with a little extra virgin olive oil, a pinch of salt and some black pepper.

Coddled egg & onions

Egg and onion is peasant food and there are few things more satisfying than this simple pairing. The key to making such modest food great is to make sure that the eggs are very fresh. Cooking onions badly is one of my pet peeves. There's a trick to it and it's not difficult; just make sure you add a good pinch of salt while they're slow cooking to break down the toughness.

Makes four small plates

6 onions
1 garlic clove
2 tbsp olive oil
70g butter
a good pinch of salt
3 sprigs of thyme
4 sprigs of flat-leaf parsley
a splash of vinegar
4 medium eggs,
   at room temperature

Peel and halve the onions then place them cut-side down and slice into half-moon slivers. Crush the garlic to a smooth paste using a mortar and pestle and set aside.

Heat the olive oil and butter in a heavy-bottomed pan. Stir through the onions with a good pinch of salt and the sprigs of thyme. Place a lid on the pan and cook on a very low heat for ten minutes until the onion is soft and sticky but without colour. Add a ladle of water if it starts to catch at all. Remove the lid and stir through the garlic. Cook for another ten minutes.

Pick the parsley off the stems, roughly chop and set aside.

Place a pan of water on the stove and bring to a gentle simmer. Add the vinegar then swirl the simmering water to create a whirlpool. Crack two eggs, each into a small glass, and lower them one at a time into the middle of the whirlpool. Check the eggs after three minutes, at which point the egg white should be set. Remove them from the pan with a slotted spoon and set them aside to drain on kitchen paper. Repeat with the remaining eggs.

Spoon the sticky onions into shallow bowls and top each portion with a soft poached egg. Serve with a scattering of parsley and seasoned to taste.

Soft-boiled egg & anchovy fingers

As a child I would hollow out my boiled egg and eat it with one large gulp, then quickly turn it upside down to pretend I hadn't eaten it. Buying the freshest eggs for this goes without saying – embarrassingly I always shuffle through the boxes before I buy to find the latest date – and perfecting the runny yolk is a must. You can use any good bread or sourdough for the anchovy soldiers, which lend a charming salty taste to cut through the richness of the gooey yolk.

Serves four

½ garlic clove, peeled
5 large good quality anchovy fillets
2 tbsp butter, at room temperature
25g Parmesan
½ tsp dried oregano
1 tsp dried parsley
black pepper, to taste
4 medium eggs, at room temperature
6 thick slices of bread

Using a mortar and pestle or food processor, pound or blitz the garlic and anchovies together until they form a coarse paste. Dollop in the butter and blitz again or whisk for three minutes until the ingredients are fully combined.

Grate over the Parmesan and add the herbs and black pepper. Give the paste a good stir then transfer to a bowl, cover and place in the fridge until ready to use.

Turn the grill on to get hot.

Place the eggs in a pan, cover with cold water and bring to the boil over a high heat. Once the water begins to boil, reduce the heat to a gentle simmer and cook the eggs for three minutes for really soft yolks.

Toast the bread then spread one side with the anchovy paste and place on a baking tray under the hot grill for two minutes. Cut into fingers to dip into the runny yolks.

English rose veal chop

English rose veal is one of the world's finest meats. I use chopped egg and capers with it for this – a classic Italian treatment. The eggs should be soft-boiled with a runny centre, and the veal should be served pink. I always source my veal responsibly from a welfare-friendly farmer in Cornwall. I like to use large chops – 2cm thick and weighing about 250g each. They might seem huge but once you've strategically dealt with the bone, each chop yields the perfect amount of meat for a single serving.

Makes four large plates

70g stale bread
6 medium eggs,
  at room temperature
1 small bunch of
  flat-leaf parsley
2 tbsp capers, rinsed
4 anchovy fillets
1 garlic clove
4 rose veal chops,
  at room temperature
2 tbsp extra virgin olive oil
salt

Pull the bread into small pieces and blitz into rough breadcrumbs.

Place the eggs in a pan, cover with cold water and bring to the boil over a high heat. Once the water begins to boil, reduce the heat to a gentle simmer and cook the eggs for three minutes for really soft yolks.

Run the boiled eggs under cold water for a moment or two then gently bash them one by one on the kitchen counter before peeling them. They will be very soft with a fairly liquid centre. Chop them roughly and set aside in a bowl.

Pick and chop the parsley and capers to a coarse texture, then scatter over the eggs.

Put the anchovies in a saucepan on a low heat, stirring until they have almost melted. Crush, peel and finely chop the garlic and toss it through the anchovies, letting it cook for a few minutes. Fold the breadcrumbs through the anchovy-garlic mixture, stirring continuously, and allow the bread to toast slightly. Remove the pan from the heat and tip over the chopped eggs, parsley and capers. Stir everything together and set aside.

Heat a heavy-bottomed frying pan over a high heat until it reaches smoking point. Rub the veal chops with the olive oil and a little salt and place in the pan. Fry the chops for three minutes on each side. Remove them from the pan, wrap them in foil and leave them to rest for five minutes.

Once rested, unwrap the chops – they should be nice and pink in the middle – and serve with the egg mixture scattered over the warm veal.

Lemon curd

This sweet, sharp spread can go with so many things and is always better when homemade. I like lemon curd on toast and pancakes, or in the centre of a simple sponge. Try to buy unwaxed lemons that almost dent when you squeeze them, as they will be juicier than the glossy solid ones you often see on supermarket shelves. Keep them in a warm kitchen and roll them over the tabletop firmly before using to render as much juice as possible.

Makes two medium or three small jars

4 unwaxed lemons
80g butter, cubed
6 medium eggs
150g caster sugar

First sterilise the jars – just wash them, then place in the oven for ten minutes at 80°C/gas ¼ to dry and keep warm.

Zest the lemons with a very fine grater, then halve and juice them.

Place a pan of water on the heat and bring to the boil. Melt the butter in a large heatproof bowl over the simmering water.

Once the butter has melted, whisk in the eggs, sugar, lemon zest and juice. Stand over the bowl and whisk continuously until the mixture gradually thickens. Be very careful not to let the curd get too hot or it will curdle.

After whisking for about eight to ten minutes, the curd will become thick, glossy and custard-like, coating the back of a spoon evenly.

Lift the bowl off the simmering water, being mindful of the steam from the pan below. Strain the curd into the warm sterilised jars. Seal the jars and leave to cool, then store the curd in the fridge. Unopened jars should keep for up to a couple of weeks.

Custard

Before you think me a custard snob, I don't think there's anything wrong with custard made with custard powder, but the real stuff just tastes so much better. It only needs eggs, milk, cream, sugar, vanilla, a watchful eye and a little stirring.

Serves six to eight

300ml milk
200ml double cream
1 vanilla pod
6 medium egg yolks
2½ tbsp caster sugar

Pour the milk and cream into a pan. Run a knife down the centre of the vanilla pod and scrape out the seeds. Add the seeds to the milk and cream, then drop in the pod too.

Put the pan onto a medium heat and bring the contents to boiling point – it will froth a bit around the edge and shudder slightly. Remove from the heat and set aside.

Whisk the yolks and sugar together in a large bowl until pale and thick. Slowly trickle in the milk, stirring continuously.

Rinse and dry the pan. Pour the milky egg mixture into the clean pan and cook over a low heat, stirring non-stop with a flat-ended spatula to stop it catching on the bottom. Once the mixture thickens enough to coat the back of a spoon, leaving a clean line when you run your finger through it, it's ready to come off the heat.

Strain the warm custard through a fine sieve and pour into a jug or bowl. This will keep for a couple of days if you are not serving it straight away; lay a piece of cling film or baking paper directly on the surface of the custard to prevent a skin forming and place in the fridge to chill until needed.

Eggy bread & cherries

The word 'unctuous' springs to mind when I think of eggy bread. I also get very nostalgic as I started eating savoury eggy bread for breakfast as a child. But why not make this as a dessert or brunch? The French may have invented it but the Americans have a much more flexible approach to eggy bread. They eat it with everything from bacon and sausages to syrup and fruit – equally enjoyable whichever way it comes.

Makes four small plates

500g cherries, perfectly ripe
100ml apple juice
2 tsp runny honey
4 medium eggs
2 tbsp milk
4 thick slices of slightly
    stale bread
1 tbsp butter
icing sugar, to dust

Rinse the cherries under cold water and remove any stalks. Using a cherry pipper or a small paring knife, remove the stones and halve the cherries.

Plonk the cherries in a wide pan and pour over the apple juice. Trickle over the honey. Cook on a medium heat for ten minutes until the cherries start to soften, burst and collapse a little into the syrupy purple sauce.

While the cherries are cooking, beat the eggs together with the milk in a shallow bowl large enough to lay the bread flat in. Squish the bread slices into the egg mixture, turning to coat both sides. Leave them in the mixture for at least ten minutes, turning them a couple of times, until almost all the liquid has been soaked up.

Once the cherries are cooked, remove them from the heat and set aside while you fry the eggy bread. Heat the butter in a heavy-bottomed frying pan over a medium to high heat. Once the butter foams and bubbles, add the soggy bread to the pan so that the slices fit in comfortably without overlapping, frying them in batches if they won't all fit at once.

Pour any excess egg mixture over the bread in the pan while it is cooking. Turn the slices after two minutes, once they are golden and crisp underneath. Cook the other side for a further two minutes.

Eat immediately with the cherries spooned over and a dusting of icing sugar.

Maple custard tart

This is a tweak on an old-fashioned custard tart recipe. Maple syrup replaces vanilla, the classic choice, and adds an elegant oaky depth. Most importantly, when cooked, the tart should retain a slight wobble.

Serves six to eight

1 sweet pastry tart case
  (page 68)
330ml maple syrup
9 medium egg yolks
500g double cream
freshly grated nutmeg

Make the sweet pastry following the recipe on page 68 and use to line a 30cm (3cm deep) circular loose-bottom tart case.

Once the pastry case has been baked and is cooling in its tin, turn the oven down to 140°C/gas 3 (it will have been at 160°C/gas 3 to bake the pastry) and start making the filling.

Whisk together the maple syrup and yolks. Stir through the cream then pass the mixture through the fine sieve into a saucepan. Put the pan on a very low heat until the custard is warm to the touch but not hot.

Place the baked tart case, still in its tin, in the middle of a flat baking tray. Pour the custard very carefully into the tart case, stopping a few millimeters before the top. If you have a cook's blowtorch, you can use it to blast the surface very quickly to get rid of any bubbles there.

Clear the pathway to the oven to avoid any custard spillages.

Place the baking tray with the tart on it gently on the middle shelf of the oven and bake for twenty five minutes, then lower the heat to 130°C/gas 2 and bake for a further fifteen to twenty minutes until the custard is set but still has a slight wobble.

Take the tart out of the oven and finely grate nutmeg all over the surface of the set custard. Cool the tart to room temperature in its tin before turning out and slicing into wedges.

St Clement's pudding

*This is not a particularly pretty pudding once spooned onto the plate –
few British desserts are – but it's so moreish eaten hot from the oven with
plenty of cream. My grandmother used to make this for me and even as a
child I was always amazed at how quick and simple it is to prepare.*

Makes four small plates

2 unwaxed lemons
1 orange
75g butter,
   at room temperature
150g soft brown sugar
3 medium eggs, separated
50g plain flour
250ml whole milk
a pinch of salt
250ml double cream, to serve

Preheat the oven to 180°C/gas 6 and fill the kettle, ready to boil later.

Butter a heatproof baking dish (10cm x 18cm and about 5cm deep).
Zest, halve and juice the lemons and orange. Add the zest to the juice.

Whisk the butter and sugar together until pale and fluffy. Beat in the
yolks one at a time. Fold through the flour then stir through the milk
a little at a time until you have a runny batter. Add the juice and zest
of the orange and lemons.

In another bowl whisk the egg whites with a pinch of salt until they
hold firm, but not stiff, peaks. Fold through the batter in a few swipes
then pour the mixture into the buttered dish.

Turn the kettle on!

Half-fill a shallow baking tray with boiling water then lower the
pudding dish into the tray – the water should be about halfway up
the dish. Bake for forty minutes until the top is browned and set
but the pudding still has a slight wobble.

Remove the pudding from the oven and immediately spoon into
bowls, pour over the cream and serve up.

Nine

I use honey all year round and in every way imaginable. It goes with the seasons. In summer, I smother a bowl of fruit and natural yoghurt with dark runny honey for breakfast. It reminds me of holidays in Greece, memories of mellow blue skies, clear warm waters and gnarled olive trees. In winter, it's different. It becomes comforting, warming my bones and soothing my raspy throat, whether trickling it on a steaming bowl of hot porridge or using it as a simple hot drink with lemon. It doesn't seem right that something so sweet can actually be healthy too. A recent study compared it with a number of branded cough medicines and found that honey was the only thing to improve any symptoms at all. As well as soothing the throat, honey is also used to boost the immune system and fight bacteria.

A spoonful of honey is sweeter than regular table sugar so just a trickle will satisfy. There is no cholesterol or fat in honey and it's the perfect source of energy before a busy day. It is the only food that includes all the substances necessary to support life, including enzymes, vitamins, minerals and water.

There are countless kinds of honey but as a general rule, light-coloured honey is milder to taste and the darker varieties are stronger. Some of the darker honeys are slightly bitter, almost medicinal, in taste. Each distinctive flavour comes from the flowers from which the bees have drawn the nectar.

We all know and love acacia, orange blossom, chestnut and Manuka honeys. I mainly use acacia honey, with its pale golden colour and mild sweet flavour for cooking. While I appreciate Manuka and chestnut honey, they are an acquired taste. The more I eat these honeys, the more I appreciate their remarkable depth and unforgettable woodland, leather and smoky characteristics. Manuka, with its slight medicinal afternote, has strong antibacterial properties that promote healing and fight off bacteria.

Orange blossom honey can vary in colour and flavour from year to year. Mostly the flavour is sweet, with unique citrus hints. It is perfect in puddings or brushed as a glaze over meats, or even whisked through olive oil to dress leaves.

On my travels in Italy in autumn I have seen chestnuts everywhere, and I do mean everywhere. Chestnut trees abound in Italy, and at this time of year, market stalls are piled high with their crop and the smell of roasted chestnuts fills the air. And where chestnut trees abound, so does chestnut honey. This is probably why the early chill of autumn is always the time that I crave chestnut honey, perhaps because it is the perfect partner for the deeper flavours of autumn cooking.

That said, cloudy, thick, set honey is my favourite because it's not quite as sickly-sweet as other honey and has a waxy, velvet quality that coats your mouth and lingers. There's nothing better than this sticky honey spread over buttery seeded toast.

Honey always reminds me of my grandma. She is a honey lover. Totally obsessed. Everything I give her is honey-related – honey lip balms, beeswax candles, honeycomb and different varieties of honey. When I was younger there was often a dribble of honey on her kitchen bench and even her kisses smelt of honey.

It is so worrying that we have seen such a rapid decline in the honey bee population. People forget that honey bees have been around for millions of years and they are the only insect that makes food eaten by man. We cooks just cannot do without this endlessly useful substance in the kitchen. One of its miraculous qualities is that it never goes off and so it helps lengthen the lifespan of anything you cook.

Honey makes all the difference in baking in particular. Cakes and bread recipes that use honey rather than sugar stay moister for longer. And unlike sugar, honey adds layers of flavour and provides a more subtle degree of sweetness. This is why it's so flexible, and such an important part of my larder, even though it makes my shelves sticky.

Courgette, Pecorino & honey

Very few dishes taste so good and look so beautiful at the same time. This recipe came about when we were trying to think of something to do with the trimmings left over from zucchini fries, because in my kitchen as little as possible goes in the bin. Chargrilling is simple and adds a whole new depth of flavour to a raw vegetable that can otherwise be quite bland. The sweet honey tames and complements the salty Pecorino. Remember, you don't need to mess around with good ingredients.

Makes two small plates

3 small courgettes
a pinch of salt
extra virgin olive oil
30g aged Pecorino Romano
runny honey

Place a griddle pan on a high heat.

While it heats up, slice the courgettes on an angle into medium-large chunks. Put them in a bowl, add a pinch of salt and a drop of olive oil and run your hands through to coat them lightly. Lay them in the hot pan and don't be tempted to move them until they have black char lines. Turn them over and cook for another couple of minutes to chargrill the other side.

Using a peeler, shave the Pecorino into a bowl, tip in the courgettes straight from the griddle and mix well. Season to taste with salt. Lavishly trickle over a small drizzle of honey to coat the courgettes lightly while they are still warm, in order to intensify the flavours and bind everything together.

Tumble onto small plates and eat while still slightly warm.

Quail & roasted radishes

Quail is simple and quick to prepare, but never fails to impress. I'd probably describe myself as a classic cook in the Italian style, but I'm always adding little variations that show my English origins. The radish here is an unusual combination, adding a wonderful pepperiness, crunch and bright pink colour to the plate. Radishes are normally eaten raw but are even more delicious roasted, mellowing and becoming sweet and sticky.

Makes two large plates

Preheat the oven to 200°C/gas 7.

2 quails
1 garlic clove
5 sprigs of thyme
extra virgin olive oil
1 bunch of radishes
  with leafy tops
1 tbsp honey
salt
juice of 1 unwaxed lemon

Prepare the birds: with sturdy kitchen scissors, snip down each side of the quail's backbone and throw the spine away or keep it for the stockpot. Turn the quail over, breast-side up, and push down hard on the breastbone with the heel of your hand to flatten it. Remove the spine with a paring knife by carefully running the knife around the bone.

Use the flat of your knife to bash the garlic clove, discarding the peel. Rub the garlic, a couple of sprigs of thyme and a little olive oil over the quail and leave them in a covered bowl in the fridge for as long as you can wait, preferably overnight.

When you're ready to cook, take the quail out of the fridge to come to room temperature.

Place a pan of water on to boil. Wash the radishes and remove the leaves, but keep hold of them for later. Plunge the radishes into the boiling water and cook them for five minutes, or until you can easily slide a knife into them. While the radishes are boiling, put a roasting tray into the oven to heat up.

Drain the radishes and tip them straight onto the heated roasting tray. Pour over the honey and a tablespoon of oil and scatter over the remaining thyme sprigs and a pinch of salt. Roast the radishes for ten to fifteen minutes until they're soft, caramelised and have taken on some colour.

While the radishes are roasting, put the griddle pan on a high heat. Sprinkle the quail with a generous pinch of salt and a little olive oil. Lay them skin-side down on the hot griddle for a couple of minutes

until they have nice char lines. Then turn them and chargrill them on the other side for another couple of minutes. Remove the quail from the pan, wrap them in foil and let them rest for five minutes. Keep all the resting juices from the tin foil parcel.

In a bowl, mix the sticky radishes and their leaves with a little olive oil, a pinch of salt and the resting juices. Squeeze over lemon juice to taste. Fold through with your hands and plate warm bundles of dressed radishes and leaves. Top with the quail and the meaty juices.

Fried Provolone
& chestnut honey

Chestnut honey has a strong taste and an almost medicinal tang, but the flavour is extraordinarily good if used sparingly. It works especially well over fried Provolone cheese. Fernando, one of my chefs, introduced me to this mild rubbery Italian cheese at Polpetto. It holds its shape while frying but has a pleasing comedy stringiness when bitten into.

Makes six to eight small plates

500g Provolone, in a block
2 medium eggs
1 tbsp milk
50g plain flour
300g polenta
1l vegetable oil, for frying
a pinch or two of salt
chestnut honey, to taste
2 unwaxed lemons, in wedges

Take the cheese and cut it into 1cm-thick pieces. It tends to come in a large round block, so it's best to cut it into roughly triangular slices.

In a bowl, beat the eggs and milk until well combined. Spread the flour on a plate, season with salt and pepper and turn it through with your fingers. Pour the polenta onto another plate.

Dredge the cheese in flour, dip into the egg and then roll it in the polenta, tossing it around until it's completely coated. Place the coated cheese in a single layer on a plate and pop in the freezer for at least ten minutes.

Heat the oil in a large heavy-bottomed saucepan over a medium heat for about ten minutes until it reaches 170°C–180°C. If you don't have a cooking thermometer, drop in a small piece of bread to test whether the oil is hot enough: the bread should come out crispy within minutes.

Lower in the coated slices one by one so as not to overcrowd the pan, as this would make the oil temperature drop. If the cheese bobs up to the surface, push it down with a spoon. Cook for about three minutes until evenly browned with a soft centre – you may see the cheese beginning to burst through the corners, or simply give it a squeeze to make sure that the centre is soft. Lift the cheese out with a slotted spoon and place on kitchen roll to drain and absorb excess oil.

Divide between the plates, sprinkle over a little salt and trickle over honey to taste. Eat immediately, served with lemon wedges to squeeze over.

Roasted pork shoulder & rhubarb

You need time to roast meat well; the more time the better. Overnight is ideal. Slow cooking results in moist meat that collapses off the bone. The bright pink rhubarb lifts this dish, adding a necessary astringency that cuts through the fat.

Makes six large plates

2 tbsp fennel seeds
2kg bone-in shoulder of
    pork, skin on
a few pinches of salt
2 onions
2 carrots
2 sticks of celery
1 bulb of garlic
4 fresh bay leaves
600ml water or vegetable stock

For the lentils:
1 onion
2 celery sticks
2 tbsp extra virgin olive oil,
    plus 1 tbsp
1 fresh bay leaf
2 sprigs of thyme
a pinch of salt
2 garlic cloves
300g Puy lentils
600ml water, chicken
    or vegetable stock

For the rhubarb:
10 sticks of rhubarb
zest and juice of
    2 unwaxed oranges
2 tbsp honey
3 sprigs of thyme

Preheat the oven to 220°C/gas 9. In a hot dry pan, toast the fennel seeds for two minutes until fragrant and then grind them to a coarse texture using a mortar and pestle.

Place the pork on a chopping board, skin-side up. Score the skin using a small sharp knife to cut lines finger-width apart – cut through into the fat, but not so deeply that you cut into the pink flesh.

Rub the salt and fennel seeds over the scored skin. Turn the shoulder over and season the underside of the meat with salt and pepper (I use a few pinches of each). Pop the shoulder skin-side up in a large roasting tray and place in the oven for twenty minutes until the skin has started to puff up and turn golden.

While the pork is cooking, peel and roughly chop the onions, carrots and celery. Break the garlic bulb into cloves with your hands and bash the cloves open with the flat of your knife.

Take the pork out of the oven, wedge the vegetables under the shoulder, rub over the bruised garlic cloves and scatter over the bay leaves. Pour over the water or stock. Tightly wrap the tray in foil, place back in the oven at 150°C/gas 3 and roast for five hours (or, for best results, overnight).

About an hour before the pork is due to come out of the oven (or about an hour and a half before you want to serve, if you cooked the meat overnight), peel and halve the onion and roughly chop the celery for the lentils. Heat two tablespoons of oil in a heavy-bottomed pan over a medium heat. Add the onions, celery, bay leaf and thyme with a pinch of salt. Peel and crush the garlic. After the vegetables have been cooking for around eight minutes, add the garlic to the pan and cook for a further five minutes, by which time the onions and celery should be soft without having taken on any colour.

Put the lentils in a separate pan, cover with cold water, bring to the boil over a high heat and simmer for ten minutes. Drain and rinse the lentils under cold running water until it runs clean. Add the lentils to the onions and celery and stir to combine. Cover with the water or stock and cook for twenty minutes on a medium heat until soft and tender. Stir through a tablespoon of olive oil and season with salt and pepper to taste. Pop a lid on and set aside.

Remove the pork from the oven and pull off the foil. Baste the pork with the fat from the tray. The meat should just collapse at the touch of a fork. Leave the meat until cool enough to handle.

Cut the rhubarb into 7.5cm sticks, discarding the dry chopped ends and leafy tops, and place them in an ovenproof dish. Zest and juice over the oranges, trickle over the honey and scatter over the thyme sprigs. Cover the dish with tin foil and place in the oven for eight minutes, or until the rhubarb is cooked through without being squidgy or falling apart – remember it carries on cooking after you remove it from the oven so it's always better to under- rather than overcook.

Remove the pork from the bone, put the meat in a bowl and cover it with foil. Carefully spoon away any fat from the stock in the roasting tray that the pork cooked in. Pass the stock through a fine sieve over a pan, squeezing all the flavour out of the caramelised vegetables. Place the pan on the hob over a high heat and bring the liquid to the boil. Let it simmer for a few minutes, stirring constantly with a wooden spoon to scrape up all those sticky bits on the bottom of the pan. When you've got a nice dark gravy, pour it over the meat pieces.

Ladle the lentils into shallow bowls, topple over generous spoonfuls of the torn pork and juices and top with a few sticks of rhubarb.

If you cook the pork overnight, the next morning remove it from the oven and baste with the fat from the tray. Once the meat is cool enough to handle, pick it off the bone, place in a bowl, pour over the cooking juices, cover and store in the fridge until needed. Then later, while you're cooking the lentils, simply place the meat in a roasting tray along with the juices, cover with foil and reheat for fifteen to twenty minutes at 180°C/gas 6. Once the pork has reheated, remove from the oven and turn the heat down to 150°C/gas 3 for the rhubarb.

Guinea fowl, raisins & honey with wet polenta

The taste of guinea fowl is somewhere between chicken and pheasant. It's less gamey game, if you like. Ask your butcher to joint it, as you won't want the hassle. Cook it slowly so that it's incredibly tender. It's quite pretty too as the honey, raisins and wine mellow and make an amber puddle on the sloppy polenta.

Makes four small plates (or two large portions if you're very hungry)

For the guinea fowl:
2 onions
extra virgin olive oil
salt
3 garlic cloves
2 sprigs of thyme
2 fennel bulbs
1 guinea fowl, jointed
120g raisins, or sultanas
500ml white wine
500ml chicken stock
2 tbsp honey

For the polenta:
1 onion
1.25l milk
2 bay leaves
4 black peppercorns
80g butter
100g quick-cook polenta
a pinch of salt

Preheat the oven to 160°C/gas 4.

Peel and halve the onion for the polenta. Pour the milk into a saucepan with the halved onion, bay leaves and peppercorns and bring up to a gentle simmer. Remove from the heat and leave to cool and infuse.

Peel and slice the onions for the guinea fowl. Heat a glug of oil in a heavy-bottomed casserole pan. When it's hot, stir in the onions with a pinch of salt and leave them to sweat for ten minutes with the lid on.

While waiting for the onions to soften, peel the garlic and slice into thin pieces. Add it to the onions with the thyme sprigs, stir to combine and cook for five minutes to mellow the harsh garlic flavour.

Halve and trim the fennel bulbs. Cut into thick slices and fold through the onions.

Place a frying pan on a high heat with a little oil. Rub salt over the guinea fowl and lay it, skin side down, in the pan to fry until golden brown. You're just going for colour here, not actually cooking it through. As soon as the guinea fowl is richly coloured, transfer the joints to the pan with the onions and add the raisins, wine, stock and honey. Put the lid on the casserole, put it in the oven and leave it to cook slowly for forty minutes.

Ten minutes before you are due to remove the guinea fowl from the oven, make the polenta. Strain the milk, discarding the bay leaves, peppercorns and onion, then return the milk to the saucepan. Put the saucepan on a medium heat and add the butter. When the butter has melted, very slowly whisk in the polenta and, turning down the heat, whisk rapidly until the granules have disappeared and all the liquid has been absorbed. Stir through a sprinkle of salt and set aside with a lid on to keep warm.

When the guinea fowl comes out of the oven you might want to skim the top with a ladle if there is a lot of fat. Spoon the wet polenta into shallow bowls and place a couple of pieces of guinea fowl on top, along with a few spoonfuls of the juices and some sticky vegetables.

Cherries, ricotta & honey

A modest, effortless concoction of summer ingredients, which will have your cheeks bulging like a hamster's, filled with cherries.

Makes four small plates

500g ripe cherries
250g sheep's ricotta
2 tbsp runny honey

Rinse the cherries under cold running water in a colander, keeping the stalks attached. Drain off all the water.

Whip the ricotta with the honey until light and creamy, and serve in dollops with the cherries.

Honey tart with clotted cream

Everyone loves the classic treacle tart – always ultra-sweet and extra-chewy. However, I think it works even better with honey precisely because it's not so sickly sweet. There's more variety and depth of flavour. You'll probably need to use a runny honey but you will be able to vary the taste by choosing different kinds. It's not essential, but I would recommend white sourdough for the breadcrumbs – this is a great way to use up leftover bread. This is best eaten straight from the oven with a spoonful of cool clotted cream, but I also like it a few days old, when the pastry has lost its crunch and has become a little soggy from the seeping honey.

Serves six to eight

*⅔ batch of sweet pastry
    (page 68)*
250g stale bread
1 x 458g jar of runny honey
200g golden syrup
2 unwaxed lemons

Make a sweet pastry using two-thirds of the quantities on page 68 and use the pastry to line a 24cm (2.5 cm deep) circular loose-bottom tart case. Follow the recipe up to the point where you fill the chilled lined case with baking beans, but this time only blind bake for ten minutes until the pastry looks set and dried but is not fully cooked.

While the pastry is blind baking, tear the bread into large chunks, wedge them into a food processor and pulse until it becomes a coarse crumb.

Pour the honey and golden syrup in a large pan and warm through over a low heat until melted and combined. Zest and juice the lemons, add to the honey syrup and stir through. Finally, fold the breadcrumbs into the mixture.

Lift the paper out of the tart case and dry out the base of the tart in the oven for a couple of minutes. Remove from the oven and turn the heat up to 180°C/gas 6 (it will have been at 160°C/gas 3 to bake the pastry).

Pour the sticky syrup carefully into the tart case, stopping a few millimeters before the top. Place the tart on the middle shelf of the oven and bake for fifteen to twenty minutes until set and firm to touch.

Slice while warm and eat with custard or a spoonful of clotted cream.

Semolina cake

Semolina pudding always reminds me of terrible school dinners – that vile, sloppy, pale, coarse paste with jam on top. It took me a while to forgive semolina, but then I realised how incredibly useful it can be. It has a granular texture that works well in cakes because it absorbs and carries more flavour than flour. Let the cake sit in its syrupy juices for as long a possible so that it soaks up the wonderful qualities of the honey.

Serves twelve

butter, for greasing
3 unwaxed blood oranges
340g floral honey
2 tsp rose syrup
350ml water
100g blanched almonds
6 medium eggs
200g caster sugar
125g fine semolina
225ml Greek yoghurt
1 handful of slivered almonds

Preheat the oven to 180°C/gas 6 and butter a 23cm round deep cake tin.

Begin by zesting and juicing the oranges. Combine the orange juice and zest with the honey, rose syrup and water in a heavy-bottomed saucepan and bring to the boil. Let the mixture simmer over a low heat for twenty-five minutes or until the syrup coats the back of a spoon. Remove from the heat and let it cool.

While the syrup is simmering, toast the blanched almonds on a dry baking tray for three minutes then set aside to cool.

Separate the egg yolks and whites into two clean medium-sized bowls. Whisk the egg whites together with half the caster sugar until they form stiff peaks. Using the same whisk (to save washing up), whisk the rest of the sugar into the egg yolks until they are pale and thick enough to hold a ribbon of mixture on the surface for a few moments.

Grind the almonds using a pestle and mortar until they have a coarse texture, then tip into a bowl and stir through the semolina and yoghurt. It will look like a thick lumpy paste.

Fold the whisked egg yolks through the semolina mixture little by little to loosen it, then gently fold in the fluffy whites, being careful not to knock the air out of the batter.

Pour the mixture into the prepared tin, scatter the slivered almonds over the top and bake for twenty-five to thirty minutes until golden brown and a knife poked into its centre comes out clean.

The moment the cake comes out the oven, pour as much syrup over as the cake will absorb and leave it to cool, still in the tin. Every so often feed the cake with more syrup.

You should leave the cake soaking away in its syrup for as long as possible before serving – at least a couple of hours – as the flavour will improve.

Poached fruit in red wine & honey

There's nothing more beautiful to me than plump ripe fruits gently simmering away in a pan, collapsing and bobbing in their juices. I love the versatility of poached fruit, whether it's poured over yoghurt, day-old cake, ice cream or jelly.

Serves four

1l red wine
100ml ginger wine
6 heaped tbsp honey
2 black peppercorns
1 cinnamon stick
1 unwaxed orange
2 ripe peaches
150g cherries
100g strawberries
100g raspberries

Put the wines, honey, peppercorns and cinnamon stick in a medium saucepan over a low heat, and use a vegetable peeler to add a few pieces of orange peel. Warm the mixture slowly to dissolve the honey then bring the crimson wine to a rolling boil for five to eight minutes.

While the liquor is simmering, bring a small pan of water to the boil and plop in the peaches. Remember to mark a shallow cross on their bottoms before they go in. After a few minutes, remove the peaches, douse them in cold water and peel back their furry skin. It should come away quite easily.

Now cut them in half and remove the stone. While you're at it, pip the cherries and hull the strawberries leaving them with as much of their natural shape as possible.

Take the liquor pan off the heat and add the peach halves and cherries. Cover with a piece of greaseproof paper and a plate to weigh it down and leave to cool.

Once cool, add the raspberries and strawberries and leave everything to marinate at room temperature for a couple of hours before you serve.

Barley ice cream with honey-roasted grapes

Barley is more popularly used in stews and soups, however during a trip to New York I came across a cornflake ice cream at a restaurant called Momofuku, and that inspired this recipe. The ice cream has a wonderful ricey, wholesome taste, which works perfectly with the sticky, plump, honeyed grapes.

Makes four small plates

300g pearl barley
125ml milk
750ml double cream
1 tbsp malt extract
10 medium egg yolks
175g caster sugar

For the grapes:
1 large bunch seedless red grapes
1 tsp extra virgin olive oil
2 tbsp runny honey
4 sprigs of thyme
a pinch of salt

Preheat the oven to 180°C/gas 6. Toast the barley on a tray for five minutes in the oven and set aside.

In a heavy-bottomed pan, warm the milk, cream, barley and malt extract over a medium heat to just below boiling point.

Whisk the yolks and sugar in a large bowl until pale, fluffy and thick enough to hold a ribbon on the surface of the froth. Pour the hot milk and cream little by little over the fluffy yolks, stirring non-stop. Return the mixture to the pan and simmer gently, stirring constantly to stop the custard turning into scrambled egg.

When the custard is thick enough to coat the back of the spoon – I run my finger along the back to see that a line stays – it is ready. Remove from the heat, pour into a container and cover with the cling film directly on the surface of the custard so that it doesn't form a skin. Chill in the fridge for two hours to infuse.

Strain the custard through a fine sieve, pounding with a ladle to squeeze out as much of that barley flavour as possible. Discarding the gloopy barley, pour the strained custard into an ice cream machine and churn until frozen. Alternatively, pour the mixture into a shallow tray and freeze for thirty minutes, then take it out and whisk through before returning it to the freezer. Whisk and refreeze three or four times until smooth and set.

Turn the oven up to 200°C/gas 7. Pull the grapes off their stalks, rinse them under cold running water and pierce them a few times with the tip of a knife. Place the grapes on a baking tray, drizzle over the olive oil and honey, sprinkle over the picked thyme leaves and salt and give the tray a shake to combine. Pop in the oven for fifteen to twenty minutes until the grapes blister and caramelise. Scoop a ball of the ice cream and place on the warm grapes to serve.

Hokey pokey

This is like a homemade Crunchie bar, only far better in my opinion as it uses honey rather than golden syrup. Hokey pokey is a Cornish term for honeycomb. It is exciting to make as the melted sugars smoke and bubble up like molten rock. It's better to make this in small batches, otherwise after a while it loses its crunch and goes soggy. I like to serve this broken over ice cream, dipped in chocolate or even paired with a rich chocolate tart.

Makes a small baking-trayful

2 tbsp golden syrup
2 tbsp honey
100g caster sugar
1½ tsp bicarbonate of soda

Line a baking tray with a sheet of greaseproof paper.

Pour the syrup and honey into a large pan, add the sugar and place on a low heat until the sugar dissolves. Stir the mixture a little but don't overdo it or it will crystallise. It'll soon boil like crazy, so make sure you don't put your fingers anywhere near it! Keep the pan over the heat until the syrupy mixture turns a deep terracotta colour.

Reduce the heat to a low heat and whisk in the bicarbonate of soda, giving it a good stir to combine, then quickly pour the mixture into the prepared tray.

Leave to cool and set thoroughly, then bash into bite-sized pieces.

Gooseberry & honey fool

I get really excited when I spot the little punnets of gooseberries in the market in the first days of July. They're only around briefly in the summer, and vary in colour from pale green to yellow and even burgundy. Wincingly sharp and tart, they definitely need sweetening. However, they are perfect for making sauces, puddings, jam, jelly and even wine. Gooseberry fool is one of my favourite summer puddings, and is a classic. The gentle floral notes of the honey in this dessert blend and mellow perfectly with the gooseberries.

Makes four small plates

400g gooseberries
3 tbsp honey
250ml double cream

Top and tail the gooseberries with a small paring knife. Put the gooseberries and honey in a stainless steel pan and stew them over a very low heat until the gooseberries pop, burst and collapse. Gently fork the berries to crush them lightly. They will give off a lot of liquid when cooked so don't be tempted to add any. If there is too much liquid, simply strain the fruit and keep the syrup for topping yoghurt or porridge in the morning.

Place the cooked gooseberries in a bowl and leave to cool in the fridge.

In a large bowl whisk the cream to soft peaks. Gently fold through the cold gooseberries to marble the cream and fruit together, resisting the temptation to stir, then spoon the fool into bowls and eat.

Honeyed panna cotta with pine nut crumble

One of the most popular desserts on Polpetto's menu, my take on the Italian 'cooked cream' has honey, which adds warmth and floral tones to the cream without being overly powerful, while the crumble lends a crunchy texture.

Makes five small plates

sunflower oil, for greasing
475ml double cream
3 tbsp honey
1 vanilla pod
3 gelatine leaves
100ml whole milk
1½ tbsp brandy

For the pine nut crumble:
130g unsalted butter
50g caster sugar
110g plain flour
30g rice flour
a pinch of salt
50g pine nuts

Lightly grease 164ml daria moulds or little glasses with sunflower oil. Pour half the cream into a heavy-bottomed pan with the honey and bring to the boil – keep the heat low until the honey has dissolved, then turn it up so that the mixture comes to boiling point. Lower the heat again and simmer slowly until the cream has reduced by half.

Pour the remaining cream into a bowl. Scrape in the seeds from the vanilla pod and whip until the cream holds its shape. Cover the bowl with cling film and place it in the fridge.

Add the gelatine to the cold milk, making sure the leaves are fully submerged in the liquid, and leave for about five minutes. Then pour the gelatine and milk into the pan containing the warm honey-cream, add the brandy and, keeping the heat low, stir until the gelatine has dissolved. Pour the mixture into a shallow tray and leave to cool for twenty to thirty minutes in the fridge until it is a similar texture to the cream.

Now fold the whipped cream through the gelatine mixture in the tray, and pass the lot through a fine sieve. Pour into the daria moulds and leave to set in the fridge for at least two hours before serving.

Meanwhile, make the crumble. Preheat the oven to 160°C/gas 4. In a large bowl, rub together the butter, sugar, flours and a pinch of salt until you get a rough breadcrumb texture. Fold through the pine nuts.

Roll the dough between two pieces of greaseproof paper until it is as thin as the pine nuts will allow. Remove the top piece of paper and bake the dough on a baking tray for fifteen minutes until golden and firm to the touch. Set aside to cool until you are ready to serve.

Take the panna cotta out of the fridge fifteen minutes before you serve it as you don't want the desserts to become too stiff. Dip the moulds into warm water before turning the set creams onto plates and breaking over the crumble.

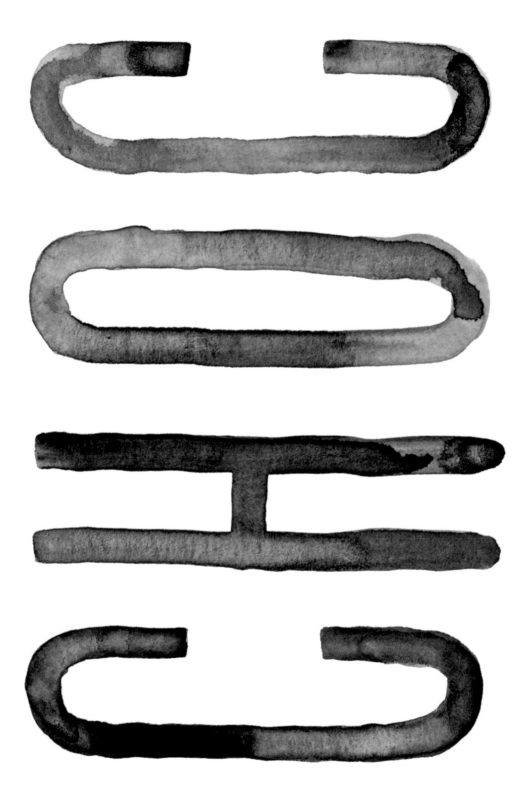

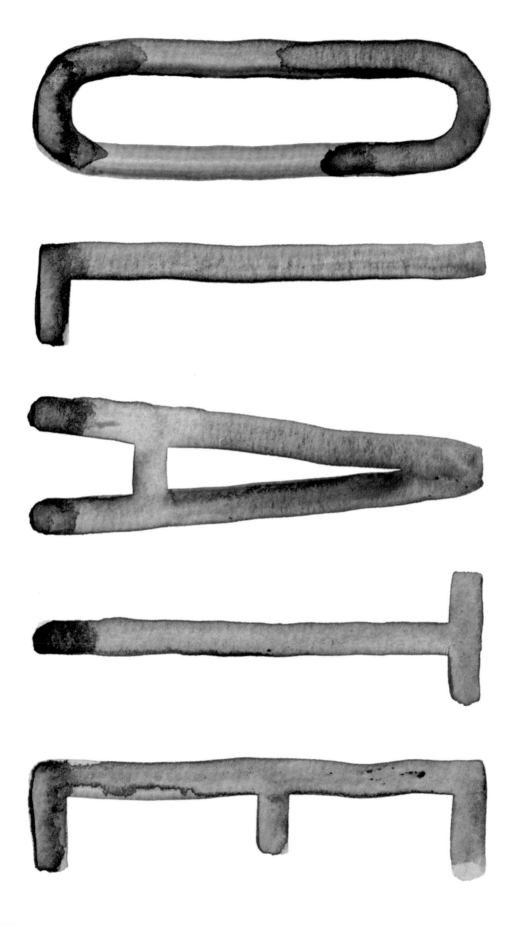

Ten

Let's face it, we all love chocolate. There probably isn't a day when I don't have a little piece. I always keep dark chocolate within easy reach in my kitchen. I have a couple of pieces at about three in the afternoon and another couple after service has ended. It makes me happy just thinking about it.

I have always been a chocolate fiend. I remember the arguments over the chocolatey spoon after baking in our house and sneakily peeling back the doors of the days yet to come on my chocolate advent calendar. Also, the laughter after I've been left with a chocolate moustache from a mug of rich hot chocolate.

Dark chocolate's health benefits have been much talked about and I'm happy to believe they are true. Good quality dark chocolate has been found to improve blood pressure, reduce the risk of a stroke and improve circulation. Now there is no longer a reason to see it as a guilty pleasure.

One of the many reasons we find chocolate so pleasing is that it tantalises the taste buds by melting on your tongue within minutes of being popped into your mouth.

We can all get a little stuck in our ways but there is more to chocolate than puddings or gooey teatime cakes. For centuries chocolate has been cooked in savoury dishes and this is still very popular in Mexico and other parts of South America. The bitter-sweetness of a good quality cocoa is perfect with gamey meats, enriching sauces, adding silky texture and mellowing strong overwhelming flavours.

I often think back to the first time I tried 'sanguinaccio' on my travels through Italy. This regional chocolate pudding shows how we have been pairing chocolate in different ways for years. The critical ingredient might just make you a little squeamish. I remember the chef peeling back the lid from a white bucket to reveal fresh blood. He then poured the glistening, thick crimson liquid into a pot as if it was just the norm before stirring in the melted chocolate. Gradually he reduced the mahogany fluid down to a thick consistency before finally adding the candied orange pieces. Once set, I took a large gulp. It tasted so luxuriously velvety on my tongue, like an extremely dense mousse but a far richer version, with a citrusy afternote. It was unforgettable.

I've also been known to combine chocolate with less obvious ingredients, and have found fennel's anise undertones to be a powerful partner. Not forgetting the more classic combinations of course, like floral honey or warming ginger.

Whether it's a small square to graze on or melted chocolate stirred through a hot chocolate pudding, don't compromise on quality. Source the best chocolate you can get your hands on. Not the milky candy bars but the pure chocolate, ground from cacao beans. Brazil, Ghana, Malaysia and Colombia all grow cacao that is distinctive in its own way, with astounding differences once you start comparing.

Chocolate brings a unique joy to the table, which is why it's on every good restaurant menu. Whether it be a bowl of chocolate rice pudding or a decadent chocolate tart, there's nothing quite like it.

Hare ragù with pappardelle

Nothing smells like braised hare when you take it out of the oven after a long night of slow cooking. It has a distinctive meaty perfume that is beautifully pungent on a cold autumn day. Don't be put off by all the preparation; it's well worth it and once the dish is in the pot, you can forget about it. As with most stews, the flavour improves with time. Jointing a hare is a messy job, so best to leave this to the butcher.

Makes four large plates

2 onions
extra virgin olive oil
a pinch of salt
1 bay leaf
2 sprigs of thyme
1 'donkey' (extra large) carrot
3 celery sticks
1 head of garlic
1 big pinch of dried chilli
1 tbsp flour
1 hare (about 1kg), jointed
1 juniper berry
375ml red wine
1 x 400g tin of whole
    plum tomatoes
250ml chicken stock
100g butter
1 tbsp cocoa powder
4 pappardelle nests
    (about 250g)
150g Parmesan

Preheat the oven to 120°C/gas 1.

Dice the onions roughly. Heat two tablespoons of olive oil in a heavy-bottomed pan (one that has a lid). Add the onions, a pinch of salt, the bay leaf and the thyme. Cover with the lid so that the onions sweat gently, keeping the heat nice and low so that they don't colour, just soften.

While the onions are softening, peel and cut the carrot and celery into medium-sized chunks. Halve the garlic head horizontally. Once the onions are soft, add the garlic and chilli and cook for a couple of minutes. Add the carrots and celery to the pan and stir everything together, replace the lid and cook for a further eight minutes. Then remove the lid, turn the heat up a little and allow the vegetables to caramelise slowly.

Heat some olive oil in a frying pan over a medium to high heat. Tip the flour onto a plate with a pinch of salt and pepper folded through it. Dust the hare joints in the seasoned flour, shaking off any excess, then fry them for a few minutes in the hot pan until browned. Place the joints in the pan with the vegetables and add the juniper berry. Pour over the red wine and let it bubble away for five minutes. Add the tinned tomatoes and chicken stock, making sure the hare is submerged beneath the liquid. Pop the lid on again and place in the oven overnight (eight hours or longer) to slow-cook in the low heat.

In the morning, carefully take the hare out of the oven and allow it to cool a little. It will fill the kitchen with a pungent, rich, hearty smell. Take out the pieces of hare out of the pan and carefully remove the bones, leaving the meat in large chunks. Strain the vegetables and cooking sauce into a bowl – the vegetables should be so soft you can effortlessly squidge them through a colander into the sauce.

Put the sauce back into the pan with the butter and cocoa powder and whisk through on a medium heat. Let the sauce reduce down to about a third of its original volume, stirring every so often to make sure it doesn't stick to the bottom. After a few minutes it will become quite thick and glossy.

Gently stir through the picked hare meat and let everything bubble away until the meat collapses into the sauce. Make sure you check the seasoning and add more chilli and salt to taste.

Cook the pappardelle in a large pan of bubbling salted water. Drain it thoroughly and then add it to the ragù sauce with a ladle of the cooking water to loosen the mixture.

Grate some Parmesan into the pan and stir it through, then serve immediately with more grated Parmesan on top of each plateful.

Braised wild boar & turnip tops

I first ate wild boar in a beautiful little osteria in Umbria and will never forget its particular flavour – somewhere between pork and venison. Boar is ideal for slow cooking, being both hearty and nourishing. It's a more unusual meat, but well worth tracking down at your local farmers' market. Use stewing cuts like shoulder or leg for this. The Italians call turnip tops 'cime di rapa' and they are eaten mostly in southern Italy. They add an earthy bitterness that helps balance out the richness of this meat. It's always best to make this a day or so in advance and leave it to sit for the flavours to improve.

Makes eight large plates

2 onions
1 'donkey' (extra large) carrot
3 sticks of celery
5 garlic cloves
extra virgin olive oil
3 juniper berries
10 black peppercorns
5 sage leaves
6 sprigs of thyme
3 bay leaves
salt
2 tbsp plain flour
1.5kg wild boar
500g pork shoulder
250ml red wine
1 x 400g tins of plum tomatoes
300ml chicken stock
fresh nutmeg
2 tbsp cocoa powder
1 dsp redcurrant jelly
50g butter
2 bunches of turnip tops

Dice the onions, carrot and celery roughly and crush the garlic using a mortar and pestle. Heat two tablespoons of oil in a large pan on a medium heat. Add the onions, juniper berries, peppercorns, sage, thyme and bay with a pinch of salt and cook gently for ten minutes on a low heat. Stir through the garlic, celery and carrot and cook for ten minutes until soft. Tip the flour onto a plate and season with a pinch of salt and pepper folded through it.

Heat a little olive oil in a saucepan over a medium heat. While the pan is heating up, cut the meats into large chunks. Dust them in the seasoned flour, shaking off the excess, and put them in the hot pan. It's best to do this in batches so as not to overcrowd it. Try not to jiggle the meat too much. Cook the chunks of meat for a few minutes on each side until evenly coloured. Tip the meat into the pan of vegetables, stirring to combine the flavours, then pour over the wine. Bring to the boil, then lower the heat until the mixture is simmering.

Add the plum tomatoes and stock then grate over a little nutmeg and simmer covered for one hour, stirring occasionally.

Remove the lid, stir through the cocoa powder, redcurrant jelly and butter and continue to cook, uncovered, for a further two hours until the meat is very tender. In total the meat should have been cooking for about three hours. Season to taste with salt and freshly ground black pepper.

Place a pan of water with a good pinch of salt in it on a medium heat and bring to the boil. Wash the turnip tops thoroughly and drain well. Roughly chop the stalks into 5cm sticks, keeping the leaves and florets whole, and cut off and discard any tougher stalks and discoloured larger leaves. Place the chopped turnip tops in the boiling water and cook for two minutes until tender.

Spoon the stew into shallow bowls. Drain the turnip tops into a small bowl, dress with olive oil and a little salt, then drape over the steaming wild boar stew.

Chocolate & honey tart

Chocolate and honey may sound a slightly unremarkable combination, but it takes skill to master good pastry and a shiny soft ganache. This is a rich and elegant tart, perfect with coffee to finish off a meal, especially when served with hokey pokey (page 260) and a dollop of cool crème fraiche.

Serves eight to ten

1 sweet pastry tart case
  (page 68)
400g dark chocolate
  (75% cocoa solids)
75g butter
475ml double cream,
  plus extra (if needed)
2 tbsp honey

Make the sweet pastry following the recipe on page 68. Once the pastry case has been baked and is cooling in its tin, make the filling.

Break up the chocolate and cut the butter into small cubes. Place them both in a large heatproof bowl.

Warm through the cream and honey in a heavy-bottomed pan over a medium heat and bring to boiling point. Pour the hot honeyed cream over the chocolate and butter and stir until melted and combined. If at any point the mixture separates, don't panic; just stir in a splash of cold double cream to bring the mixture back.

Cover the top of the chocolate mixture with cling film directly on the surface so that a skin doesn't form, then leave to cool slightly until the mixture thickens a little – ten minutes will be long enough.

Remove the cling film and give the filling a good stir before pouring it into the empty tart case (still in its tin, just to be safe). Smooth the chocolate with the back of a spoon or swirl it for a rougher texture. Carefully remove from the tin and slice before serving.

Torta di cioccolato e amaretto

Amaretto liqueur makes this a boozy treat. The name 'Amaretto' comes from the Italian word for 'bitter' but we know it as a sweet almond-flavoured liqueur that has been paired with chocolate for years to make great desserts. Pouring the Amaretto over the biscuits and allowing them to drink up the liquor before squishing them evenly over the half-baked base is all part of the fun of making this cake. It is actually baked twice, which gives it a soft-set top and makes it intensely rich. This cake caused a real stir at Polpetto and was easily one of our most popular desserts. Using a good dark chocolate is important and I would recommend buying the best quality bar you can get your hands on. The Muscovado sugar adds a beautiful caramel note and blends into the chocolate to create layers of fudgy flavour. This is not a cake for the faint-hearted. It's very indulgent; perfect for chocoholics. I like to serve a generous helping with a spoonful of chilled crème fraiche, which adds a pleasant sourness.

Serves eight to ten

270g dark chocolate, plus 100g
240g butter
290g Muscovado sugar
5 dsp water
5 medium eggs
115g Amaretti biscuits
a pinch of salt
75ml Amaretto liqueur
cocoa powder, to dust

Preheat the oven to 180°C/gas 6. Butter and line a 23cm round cake tin.

Break up 270g of the chocolate and melt together with the butter in a heatproof bowl over a pan of barely simmering water.

While they are melting, pour the sugar and water into a small pan over a low heat. Dissolve the sugar and bring the mixture to the boil for a couple of minutes.

Remove the melted chocolate and butter from the heat and pour in the sugar syrup. Give it a stir then leave to cool down for ten minutes, as you don't want it to be so hot that it scrambles the eggs. While the mixture is cooling, separate the eggs and bash the Amaretti biscuits with the end of a rolling pin.

Once the mixture has cooled, pour in the egg yolks, add a pinch of salt and stir to combine.

Whip the egg whites until they can hold a ribbon on the surface. Fold them through the chocolate mixture carefully using a large spoon. It'll be quite a runny batter at this point.

Pour half the mixture into the cake tin and bake for thirty minutes until it has started to wrinkle away from the edges of the tin but isn't fully cooked through. Remember that this part of the cake is going to be baked again. Put the cake batter bowl (covered in cling film) in the fridge until you come to bake the other half.

While the cake is baking, pour the Amaretto over the crushed biscuits and leave them to soften and absorb the liqueur – I like this quite boozy but obviously it is a matter of personal taste so you can use less alcohol if you prefer. Smash up the 100g of chocolate and set aside. Remove the cake from the oven and leave to cool in the tin for ten minutes.

Scatter the soaked Amaretti and the chocolate shards over the cooled base and spoon the remaining batter over the top. The half-baked base will have shrunk away from the sides slightly but that's absolutely fine. Place back in the oven for fifteen to twenty minutes until a cocktail stick or knife tip comes out almost clean. Remove from the oven and leave it to cool in the tin.

When the cake is completely cool, dust with cocoa powder then slice and serve with crème fraiche.

Bread & butter pudding

*I like to use sweet Italian bread in my bread and butter pudding.
It adds richness and makes it extra special. The 'golden bread' pandoro
is especially good in this recipe. It is similar to panettone but specific
to Verona and is super-rich and buttery. It is traditionally eaten at
Christmas but is readily available in good Italian delicatessens
at any time of the year.*

Makes four to six small plates

750g pandoro
1 dsp butter
160g dark chocolate
6 medium eggs
*1 heaped tbsp Demerara
    sugar, plus extra*
a pinch of salt
100ml whole milk
485ml double cream

Cut the pandoro into thick slices and butter one side.

Layer buttered slices over the base of an 18cm long, 5cm deep
baking dish until the base is covered. Snap the chocolate into small
pieces and scatter some over the layered pandoro, reserving enough
chocolate for the other layers. Repeat this with the remaining bread
and chocolate until you have none left. Squidge the bread down a
little and set aside.

In a large bowl, beat the eggs together with the Demerara sugar
and salt, then trickle over the milk and cream. Whisk the mixture
together until all combined.

Pour half the custard mixture through a fine sieve over the pandoro,
squishing the bread down with a spoon. Cover loosely with cling film
and leave the whole thing to stand at room temperature for at least
two hours. Feed the pandoro with more of the custard every thirty
minutes until it has all been absorbed.

Preheat the oven to 180°C/gas 6 and boil the kettle.

Stand the dish in a deep roasting tin and carefully pour in boiling
water until the water level is halfway up the side of the dish. Sprinkle
over a little extra Demerara sugar and bake for twenty five to thirty
minutes until golden and set with a gentle wobble.

Rice pudding & blackberries

Rice pudding tends to be a love or hate thing, I suppose. I've always loved the stuff and I even eat the Ambrosia variety straight out of the tin. It's just so comforting. The addition of blackberries contributes a lovely tang that offsets the sweetness of the chocolatey rice.

For four to six

75g salted butter
65g soft light brown sugar
150g Vialone nano rice
1l whole milk
1 bay leaf
70g dark chocolate
150ml double cream
250g blackberries
3 tbsp water
1 tbsp caster sugar

Preheat the oven to 140°C/gas 3. Lightly butter the sides of an 18cm long, 5cm deep baking dish using some of the 75g of butter.

Place the remaining butter in a pan. Gently heat until the butter is melted and foaming then add the sugar. Stir, letting the sugar dissolve into the butter.

Tip in the rice and continue to stir, coating each grain in the sugary butter mixture. After about five minutes the rice will swell a little, but don't be tempted to stop stirring.

Pour over the milk and beat out any lumps of rice, carefully scraping the bottom of the pan to dislodge any stuck grains. Add the bay leaf, chocolate (broken in pieces) and cream. Bring to a simmer and cook for ten minutes, still stirring.

Pour the rice pudding into the buttered dish and stand it in a deep roasting tin. Boil the kettle then carefully pour the boiling water into the roasting tin until the water comes halfway up the sides of the dish. Bake in the oven for seventy-five minutes until the pudding is set but still slightly wobbly – it may need a little longer than this, but if it does, do remember to check on it regularly so that it doesn't overcook.

While the rice is baking, put the blackberries in a pan with the water and sugar and simmer over a low heat until the berries burst and collapse.

Serve the rice pudding warm rather than piping hot, with or without the skin, along with a good spoonful of the stewed blackberries.

Chocolate & ginger meringue pie

I think of my little sister whenever I work with meringue. She loved it as a child, devouring all but a few pieces of the sticky pie as soon as I had made it. Meringue can be overly sweet, but what I love about this recipe is that the sweetness is balanced out by the richness of the chocolate and fiery heat of the ginger. Making meringue can seem tricky but honestly it is a doddle. It's all about making sure that the eggs are at room temperature and having clean, grease-free equipment to achieve full-bodied stiff peaks. A swift rub of lemon over your whisk and bowl will help to remove any hidden grease. Whisking the egg whites by hand may not be the easy option, but believe me it will result in perfect meringues. The centre should be perfectly soft and chewy while the exterior is crisp and wafer-like.

Serves six or eight, depending on how greedy you want to be

1 sweet pastry tart case (page 68)
265g dark chocolate
50g butter
320ml double cream, plus extra (if needed)
3 tbsp stem ginger syrup
4 knobs of stem ginger
120g caster sugar
2 egg whites
a pinch of salt

Make the sweet pastry following the recipe on page 68. Reserve the egg whites for the meringue.

Once the pastry case has been baked and is cooling in its tin, make the filling. Break up the chocolate and cut the butter into small cubes. Place them both in a large heatproof bowl.

Warm through the cream and ginger syrup in a heavy-bottomed pan over a medium heat and bring to boiling point. Pour the hot ginger cream over the chocolate and butter and stir until melted and combined. If at any point the mixture separates, don't panic; just stir in a splash of cold double cream to bring the mixture back.

Cover the top of the chocolate mixture with cling film directly on the surface so that a skin doesn't form, then leave to cool slightly until the mixture thickens a little – ten minutes will be long enough.

Remove the cling film and give the filling a good stir before pouring it into the empty tart case (still in its tin). Smooth the chocolate with the back of a spoon. It won't fill the whole case, so don't worry. Roughly chop the stem ginger into uneven pieces and scatter them over the chocolate. Put this to one side to set.

Preheat the oven to 200°C/gas 7.

Line a baking tray with greaseproof paper and sprinkle the sugar evenly over it. Place the tray in the oven for five minutes until the sugar is hot but not melted or browned in any way.

While the sugar is heating up, make sure the bowl and whisk for the egg whites are grease-free. Whisk the whites with a pinch of salt to form stiff peaks. Remove the sugar from the oven (which you can switch off now) and tip into a heatproof jug. Trickle the sugar slowly over the egg whites while whisking, until they become glossy and hold their shape. This should only take a few minutes.

Dollop over the meringue onto the chocolate and ginger mixture in the tart case and loosely spread it to the edges of the tin with a palette knife or the back of a spoon.

Heat the grill to a high heat or use a blowtorch to cook the meringue evenly until golden, then slice and serve.

Hazelnut chocolate fondant with pickled grapes

These are like huge 'Ferrero Rocher' chocolates but with even more unctuous runny centres. The grapes add sourness to what would otherwise be an overly rich dessert. If you don't have any Moscatel wine vinegar, don't worry; you can use any other very good quality white wine vinegar. A useful tip: you can make and freeze the fondants in advance as they bake perfectly from frozen.

Makes four small ramekins

butter, for greasing

For the pickled grapes:
1 bunch of red seedless grapes
100g caster sugar
125ml Moscatel wine vinegar
50ml water
2 cloves

For the fondants:
100g hazelnuts
100g dark chocolate
100g unsalted butter
50g dark Muscovado sugar
50g golden caster sugar
2 medium eggs,
*   at room temperature*
2 medium egg yolks
100g plain flour

The day before you want to serve this, pickle the grapes. Break up the stems into nice clusters, rinse and pat dry. In a non-reactive pan (not aluminium or copper), dissolve the sugar with the vinegar, water and cloves over a medium heat and allow to bubble for a few minutes. Put the grapes into a heatproof bowl and pour the hot syrup over. Make sure the grapes are submerged then leave to cool. Once cooled, cover with cling film and leave overnight.

Preheat the oven to 180°C/gas 6. Grease four small ramekins generously with butter.

Toast the hazelnuts on a baking tray in the oven for a few minutes until they're golden brown and have a nutty smell. Tip them into a tea towel, wrap it up into a bundle so the hazelnuts don't escape and rub it on the work surface to remove the nuts from their skins. Pick out the hazelnuts and chop them quite finely so that there aren't any big lumps, but don't reduce them to dust.

Throw some chopped hazelnuts into each ramekin and shake them so that the nuts fully coat the base and sides. Repeat if you need to and tip out any excess nuts. Put the ramekins in the fridge while you make the fondant mixture.

Break up the chocolate and melt together with the butter in a heatproof bowl over a pan of barely simmering water. Once fully melted, give it a stir and set aside to cool.

Beat the sugars, eggs and egg yolks together in a big bowl until the mixture is thick enough to hold a nice big ribbon on the surface. Very delicately sieve the flour onto the egg mixture and fold it through with a big spoon, being careful not to knock out the air. Then gradually fold through the melted buttery chocolate to create a kind of sloppy batter.

Spoon into the prepared ramekins so that each is about two-thirds full, which will give them space to rise. Chill in the fridge for at least thirty minutes. If you are making these in advance, put them in the freezer at this stage and simply bake from frozen when you come to cook them, adding an extra five minutes to the baking time.

Preheat the oven to 200°C/gas 7.

Place the chilled ramekins on a baking tray and bake for ten minutes until the fondants have formed a nice crust and started to wrinkle away from the edges.

Remove from the oven and let each one sit upside-down on a small plate for a minute, to let the sides loosen. If the fondants haven't completely come away from the edges by then, run a butter knife around the sides and turn the fondants out onto the plates.

Taste a pickled grape and if they're too strongly vinegary, rinse them under cold water. Shake any clinging droplets of liquid from the grapes and serve in clusters next to the fondants.

Chocolate sorbet
& candied fennel

I drink fennel tea and like to dip dark chocolate in it, which is how I came to love this unusual combination. Candying can be tricky, but it's a labour of love. You can also dip the candied fennel in chocolate, which is delicious in itself. This sorbet is so luxuriously rich and thick, you might think it's ice cream.

Makes four small plates

For the chocolate sorbet:
250g caster sugar
750ml water
120g cocoa powder
50ml Pernod

For the candied fennel:
1 unwaxed lemon
1 bulb of fennel
100ml water
200g caster sugar

Start by making the sorbet. Dissolve the sugar in the water in a heavy-bottomed pan over a gentle heat. Once the sugar has dissolved, bring the mixture to the boil and allow to bubble until you have a light syrup. Remove the pan from the heat and gently whisk in the cocoa powder until it too has dissolved. Add the Pernod, stir once or twice so that it is incorporated, then place the pan back on the heat and whisk continuously while the mixture bubbles away for five minutes until it is the consistency of single cream. Strain the mixture through a fine sieve into a bowl and leave it to cool down.

Halve the lemon and put it in a bowl of cold water. Remove the outer skin of the fennel and cut the bulb into slices about the thickness of a pound coin. Put the slices in the cold lemon water.

Place a medium-sized pan of cold water on a high heat and bring it to the boil.

Pour 100ml water into a separate wide saucepan, add the sugar and place on a low heat. Once the sugar has dissolved, use a pastry brush dampened with cold water to clean the sides of the pan to ensure that the mixture doesn't crystallise, and remember not to stir it.

Now lift the fennel out of the lemon water and put it in the pan of boiling water to blanch for three minutes. Then, using a slotted spoon, lift the fennel slices out of the boiling water and put them straight into the warm sugar-water. Bring to a gentle simmer and allow to bubble for twenty to thirty minutes until the fennel is soft and translucent, having absorbed nearly all of the thick syrup. Use a slotted spoon to remove the fennel and transfer the slices to a wire rack to cool.

Once the chocolate mixture has cooled, pour it into an ice cream machine and churn it until frozen. Alternatively pour it into a rigid plastic container, preferably bowl-shaped, and freeze until the mixture has frozen a couple of centimetres in from the edges (this should take about an hour). Whisk to break up the ice crystals and freeze it again for another hour. Whisk, freeze and whisk again one more time, then leave until completely frozen.

Serve scoops of sorbet with a few slivers of fennel alongside.

Pear & chocolate upside-down cake

'Upside-down' cake because it's cooked upside-down. The moment of truth comes when the cake is flipped to reveal the succulent fanned pear wedges underneath. Chocolate and pears go so well together that I'm surprised they aren't combined more often – they come together beautifully in this cake. Try to use the best quality chocolate you can find and under-ripe British pears. This is one of those rare occasions in cooking when a ripe fruit will not do. The Poire William adds a naughty alcoholic kick.

Serves eight

5 under-ripe pears
180g dark chocolate
250g butter
6 eggs
175g sugar
100g ground almonds
2 tbsp Poire William liqueur

Preheat the oven to 170°C/gas 5 and grease and line a 23cm round deep cake tin.

Peel, core and cut the pears into eighths. Arrange them core-side down in a fanned circle at the bottom of the tin.

Put a pan on the heat with a little water in it and set a heatproof bowl over it. Break up the chocolate and melt together with the butter in the bowl.

While they're melting, beat the eggs and sugar together until pale and fluffy. Stir in the melted chocolate then carefully fold in the ground almonds.

Tip the batter into the tin and bake for forty-five to fifty minutes. Use a skewer to test the centre to check that it is baked through.

As soon as it comes out of the oven, pour the Poire William all over the top and leave to cool in the tin.

Bomboloni con cioccolato e finocchio

These doughnuts remind me of a holiday in Florence and the regular bellows of 'bomboloni' through the cobbled streets, where they are popular and traditionally custard-filled. Mine are filled with chocolate and rolled in fennel-seed sugar. This was an extremely popular dessert at Polpetto, where I had an annoying tendency to sing the Gipsy Kings' song 'Bamboleo' whenever the order came in!

Makes twenty-four

For the dough:
250g Italian 00 (or plain) flour
½ tbsp caster sugar
4g fresh yeast
125ml milk
25g butter
1 medium egg
a generous pinch of salt

For the chocolate filling:
100g dark chocolate
1½ tsp Muscovado sugar
1 star anise
65ml water

For the fennel sugar:
2 tbsp fennel seeds
300g caster sugar

1l sunflower oil, for frying

Begin with the dough. Place the flour, sugar and crumbled yeast in a food mixer or mixing bowl. Warm the milk in a small pan on a very low heat and add the butter so that it melts, being careful not to overheat it (the liquid should be about blood temperature). Make a well in the flour, pour in the warm liquid and add the egg and salt. Bring the mixture together with a spoon then turn onto a floured surface and knead thoroughly until the dough is as soft as a baby's bottom.

Place the dough back in the bowl, cover with a damp cloth and leave in a warm, dry place until the dough doubles in size. This should take about two hours.

In the meantime make the chocolate filling. Break the chocolate into small pieces and melt in a heatproof bowl over a pan of boiling water on a medium heat. Put the sugar, star anise and water in a small pan over a low heat and stir until the sugar dissolves. Bring the mixture to the boil for two minutes over a medium heat until it takes on a syrupy consistency. Pour the syrup into the melted chocolate and stir until the mixture is glossy and thick. Set aside to cool. Once cooled, roll the chocolate into twenty-four small marble-sized balls, ready for the bomboloni dough.

Knock the dough back and then roll it out to the thickness of a two-pound coin. Use a small cup or cutter (about 6cm in diameter) to cut out twenty-four disks.

Place a small ball of chocolate onto the middle of each disk and run a wetted finger around the edge of the dough. Pinch the edges of each disk together like a wonton, enclosing the chocolate, then roll them into balls in your hands. When all the bomboloni have been filled and rolled, place them on a floured baking tray and cover with a damp cloth. Leave in a warm place for twenty minutes to rise again until they are the size of golf balls.

While you are waiting, preheat the oven to 180°C/gas 6. Toast the fennel seeds on a baking tray in the oven for three minutes and then mix them with the caster sugar.

Heat the oil in a large heavy-bottomed pan over a medium heat for about twenty minutes until it reaches 170°C–180°C. Drop in a small piece of leftover dough to test whether the oil is hot enough: it should come out crispy within minutes.

Fry the bomboloni for three to five minutes on each side until they are golden all over. They like to bob up to the surface so you will have to push them down into the oil with a spoon. Remove them one at a time with a slotted spoon and immediately pop them into the fennel sugar, rolling them around until evenly coated. Eat them while hot.

Honey chocolate truffles

Nothing finishes off a meal better than the hit of a chocolate truffle, especially when served with a fine liqueur or coffee. Ideal as they can be rolled well in advance of serving, I make mine both at work and when I'm at home, often with the help of my niece and nephew. It's important that you use the best quality chocolate you can lay your hands on.

Makes about 500g

180ml double cream
3 tbsp floral honey
450g dark chocolate
a pinch of salt
80g butter
extra-bitter cocoa powder,
*   to finish*

Boil the double cream and honey in a saucepan over a medium heat, being careful that it doesn't bubble over. Simmer until the cream has reduced in volume by two-thirds: it will look very thick and have a slightly yellowish edge.

Break the chocolate into small pieces. Remove the cream from the heat. Add the chocolate and salt and stir until all the chocolate has melted through the cream. Add the butter and gently stir until the mixture becomes very glossy. Spoon the mixture onto a plate and leave in the fridge for a couple of hours to set and form a slight crust.

Tip the cocoa powder into a shallow bowl. Scoop up the truffle mixture with a small teaspoon and use your hands to roll it gently into rough spheres. Shake the truffles around in the cocoa powder until completely covered then chill them for fifteen minutes until set.

Acknowledgements

I will always be grateful to my family. Especially to my mum who has inspired me and nurtured my creativity throughout my life. My sister-in-law Amanda Knight has been officially 'knighted'. I'm very fortunate to have such a talented chef within the family to help perfect all the recipes. Dad isn't around now but is always with me in good times and bad. In a way this book is for him.

I have profound admiration for Russell Norman and much gratitude for his great trust in me and for his sagacious advice and enduring encouragement throughout my work. Libby Greenfield's passion for food made every day at Polpetto a pleasure.

My dear friend Scott Athorn has been part of the journey of this book from the outset. Scott contributed much-appreciated support and structure, as well as his trained journalist's eye. Many thanks to Savannah Lambis for her intelligent rational advice, military-like day-to-day organisation and for her constant positive energy that makes working with her such a joy.

I'm forever thankful for my literary agent Eugenie Furniss, who has been my champion and confidante. Her belief in me has been humbling.

I could never have hoped for a more wonderful, patient editor than Elizabeth Hallett. My thanks to the meticulous eye of my copy editor Bryony Nowell who sifted my words with her fine-tooth comb, and to everyone at Hodder, especially Alasdair Oliver and Eleni Lawrence. Many thanks, also, to Tanya Layzell-Payne and her team. I'm immensely grateful to all of the above.

Matt Willey has listened to and braved my wailing and even a few tantrums, but with no surprise he has designed a book to be proud of. I heartily thank Jason Lowe for his beautiful photography and Joe Woodhouse for all the nuts and bolts behind the scenes on those long days. A big thank you to the lovely Cynthia Inions, who made shooting this book a joy and wholeheartedly understood my broken beauty ways.

This book has been a roller coaster of emotions and without my husband Richard's constant encouragement, saintly patience and loving support this book simply wouldn't have happened. I'm very happily bound to him for that.

Page numbers in **bold** refer to photographs

First published in Great Britain in 2013 by Saltyard Books
An imprint of Hodder & Stoughton
An Hachette UK company

1

A CIP catalogue record for this title is available from the British Library

ISBN 978 1 444 73485 0
eBook ISBN 978 1 444 73487 4

Book design by Matt Willey
Typeset in Antwerp

Copy editor Bryony Nowell
Proofreaders Miren Lopategui and Laura Herring
Indexer Caroline Wilding

Printed and bound by Graphicom, Italy

Hodder & Stoughton policy is to use papers that are natural, renewable
and recyclable products and made from wood grown in sustainable forests.
The logging and manufacturing processes are expected to conform to the
environmental regulations of the country of origin.

Hodder & Stoughton
338 Euston Road
London NW1 3BH

www.saltyardbooks.co.uk